I AM
STANDING UP
True Confessions of a Total Freak Of Nature

Luke Lang

ZONDERVAN®

ZONDERVAN.com/
AUTHORTRACKER
follow your favorite authors

▌ZONDERVAN®

I AM Standing Up: True Confessions of a Total Freak of Nature
Copyright © 2009 by Luke Lang

Requests for information should be addressed to:

Zondervan, *Grand Rapids, Michigan 49530*

ISBN 978-0-310-28325-6

Cover design by SharpSeven Design
Interior design by Mark Novelli, IMAGO MEDIA

Printed in the United States of America

09 10 11 12 13 14 • 23 22 21 20 19 18 17 16 15 14 13 12 11 10 9 8 7 6 5 4 3 2 1

DEDICATION

Heavenly Father, every day I experience more of your creativity, grace, and redeeming love. You are truly too wonderful for words. I pray that somehow you would be glorified in my simple story.

For Diana, who had the courage, faith, and humor to see beyond the surface. I love you!

Delanie, you are an amazing young lady. I'm so proud of you, and I'm honored to be your freaky little father.

Really BIG thanks to my family and friends for letting me share their stories as I've shared mine.

Thank you to the fine folks at Youth Specialties and Zondervan. You are simply the coolest and most talented group of people on the planet. It has been a blast working with you. Thanks for getting it.

TABLE OF CONTENTS

The Big Intro: My Life...a Real Short Story   7

Chapter 1: The Birth—and Narrow Escape—of a Freak   13

Chapter 2: Boy Scout Camp—or My Personal Hell   20

Chapter 3: Saved by a Wedgie   25

Chapter 4: Jimmy   29

Story Time with Uncle Luke: "Otis Porkmeyer"   34

Chapter 5: Potty Mouth   37

Chapter 6: Second-String King   42

A Mindless Poetry Slam with Uncle Luke   51

Chapter 7: Training Band?   53

Chapter 8: The Single Most Important Thing I Ever Learned in English Class   58

Story Time with Uncle Luke: "I Like My Pants"   63

Chapter 9: Everybody Was Kung Fu Fighting   66

Chapter 10: Blind Date   70

Chapter 11: The Return of Potty Mouth   76

Chapter 12: The Peach Cobbler Story   80

Chapter 13: Chasing Jupiter   86

Chapter 14: Squirrels and Ducks, Oh My!   90

Story Time with Uncle Luke: "Norbert Knows His Nose"   94

Chapter 15: Black and Blue Angels   97

Chapter 16: A Rambling Conversation with Myself   102

Chapter 17: Allow Me to Rant   106

Chapter 18: Soiling Myself Shogun Style   109

Story Time with Uncle Luke: "Noah and His Amazing Bumps"   114

Chapter 19: Cow Manure and Grace   116

Chapter 20: That's It...I'm Putting Myself up for Adoption!   121

Chapter 21: Twister   127

Story Time with Uncle Luke: "The Thing Under My Bed"   131

Chapter 22: Lessons from Dad   134

Chapter 23: The Prayer of Saint Pete   139

Chapter 24: The World's Shortest Self-Help Book   143

Chapter 25: The Art of Conformity   144

Chapter 26: Freak of Nature   149

Chapter 27: I AM Standing Up!   151

"They will see in our history
the faithful love of the LORD."
(Psalm 107:43, NLT)

the big intro

My Life...
a Real Short Story

Hi, my name is Luke, and I have a confession to make. (You probably guessed from the cleverly worded subtitle.) Come a little closer. This isn't easy for me. My deep, very personal confession is—brace yourself; this isn't pretty—I am a total freak of nature. (I know you probably figured that out...again that clever subtitle thing.)

It's true. I am a walking, talking, one-man freak show. Let me explain. For starters it's a genetic thing. I'm five feet, one inch tall. So I'm basically the height of an average fifth grader, but I'm also a chubby little dude, pretty much the width of an average sumo wrestler. It's an interesting combination. Also, as I've gotten older, I've lost most of my hair.

Are you getting the picture? I'm basically everything physically undesirable about a man rolled up into one chunky little package. I'm the *GQ* anti-cover boy. As if that weren't enough, I'm also blind in one eye, which means I don't have a whole lot of depth perception. This results in my bumping into things and falling down frequently—which is fun at parties but a pain in real life.

But wait—there's more. I'm freakishly uncoordinated, and I have an amazing gift for embarrassing myself by saying or doing stupid things. In school I was the classic underachiever. I never really applied myself, and my grades definitely reflected that.

As a result of all of this, my life has been a nonstop series of misadventures and mishaps—many of which you're about to read. All of these factors combined to make me a social, genetic freak. As I was growing up, I never liked myself. I hated what I looked like. I hated the undeniable fact that I was different than everyone else on the planet. I never fit into any group. I was left out and left behind. The few times I didn't feel invisible, I wished I was.

Then something happened that forever changed my life. I discovered my purpose and my passion. I never felt the acceptance and significance I craved until I came into a relationship with Jesus Christ. I realized God loves the freak, the geek, and the weak. I'm extremely glad because I've been all three. In time I came not only to accept who I am but also to celebrate it. I realized the Creator custom-designed me for the life I have. I've been able to reach people and do things I wouldn't have been able to do if I was normal. God has most used the very things that make my life different.

A passage from the Bible gives my life some clarity. I also want to use these Scriptures as a bit of a backdrop for the stories that follow. The soundtrack for my life is 1 Corinthians 1:26-29, and it reads, "Brothers and sisters, think of what you were when you were called. Not many of you were wise by human standards; not many were influential; not many were of noble birth. But God chose the foolish things of the world to shame the wise; God chose the weak things of the world to shame the strong. God chose the lowly things of this world and despised things—and the things that are not—to nullify the things that are, so that no one may boast before him."

If you've ever felt like a misfit, an outsider, an underachiever, a loser, or a freak, I've got some comforting news for you. You're not alone. If you read the Bible, you'll find you're in pretty good company. The Scriptures are full of misfits and outcasts. It's one big flock of freaks.

But something has happened in the church during the last few decades. We've become obsessed with image. Many Christians present this shiny, prefabricated facade that our lives are perfect. We try to act like once we become Christ followers, all our problems magically disappear. We appear to have perfect lives with perfect families. We have perfect teeth and perfect complexions. Everything is just...perfect.

Not only is this a big ugly lie, but it also keeps people from becoming Christians. Because most people can't even relate. They know they can't be perfect like they think we are. Why can't we just be honest?

The Bible is an amazingly honest book. Its stories include some seriously dysfunctional families and messed-up people, and these are the people God chose to use. God didn't have to include all of their weirdness in the Bible, but he did because it gives us hope. The truth is, most Christians have very imperfect lives. Stuff happens, and we can be pretty messed up. But we've fallen in love with Jesus—and that makes all the difference in our lives.

I hope to single-handedly disband all the falsehoods of perfection by sharing some of the issues and events of my little life. I also hope my life gives you hope. My sincere prayer is that through the goofy little stories in this book, you'll see the creativity and redeeming power of God.

I've tried to give some kind of spiritual application with most of these stories, but some are included for the sole purpose of making you laugh and helping you feel a little better about your life. All of these stories are true, and they all point to the very real fact that God loves me even when I do stupid stuff. I want you to read this book and realize that the living and loving God custom-designed you, too. He did it on purpose, for a purpose. I know that might sound like a cheesy bumper sticker slogan, but it's really the truth. I pray that no matter what stage of your life journey you're at, you'll discover the truth about who God is and the truth about who you are—and the truth will set you free.

Welcome to the freak show!

—Luke

But wait! There's more. Let me give you fair warning. You'll also find, sprinkled throughout these pages, several brief interludes titled "Story Time with Uncle Luke." These are simply some pretty goofy poems and children's stories I wrote, usually late at night. They're a little twisted, but they're fairly harmless. They are included to help you get in touch with your inner seven-year-old.

You're also going to find scattered throughout the book several cartoons I've drawn. Don't look for any deep theological significance in the cartoons—they're included for the sole purpose of hopefully making you laugh, which I think is actually one of the most spiritual things you can do. They'll also give you a little added insight into my warped worldview.

The Big Intro: My Life...a Real Short Story

chapter one
The Birth—and Narrow Escape—of a Freak

This is a true story—it happened exactly the way I describe it, I promise.

Once upon a time there was a young girl who had big plans. She was from an all-American family. She had three big sisters and one little brother. They lived in a nice house on the right side of town. Her dad owned his own successful business. Her mom stayed at home, baked cookies, and wore an apron. Her parents also had big plans for her future. She would go to college, maybe become a teacher, eventually settle down with a respectable man, and live a safe, comfortable, predictable life.

But then something happened. She met *him*. He was handsome and mysterious. She fell in love. But her family didn't approve. He was a high school dropout from the wrong side of town. He drove fast and hung out with a really rough crowd. He'd been in the Army. He had sideburns and a tattoo—although it wasn't a very good tattoo. It was supposed to be a ferocious panther. Instead it looked like a really imposing sweet potato. As far as her folks were concerned, he was bad news.

But the boy and girl didn't care because they were in love. They had big plans for their future. They would date for a few years, and then once he got a good, high-paying job, they would get married. They were so in love. Then late one passion-filled November night, they consummated their love in the backseat of a Chevrolet. A few weeks later the girl found out she was pregnant.

Their big wedding plans sped up a bit, and they ended up eloping on a blustery winter evening. Their big plans had changed. Suddenly, they had big plans for a family: a little house with a nursery, a crib, toys, and a big backyard with plenty of room for a child to grow up.

Finally, the time came. Their baby was on the way. The boy drove the girl to the hospital. Because of some really heavy sedatives, she doesn't remember a lot about the actual birth.

All she remembers was coming out of her drug-induced slumber to find several very somber-looking doctors surrounding her bed. They explained to her that there were complications. Her baby was sick...really sick. She had delivered a boy, but he was born with fluid on the brain. The doctors told her it was very unlikely her child would survive the next 24 hours. And if by some remote chance he lived, he'd be severely mentally and physically handicapped. He would basically be a vegetable and wouldn't live past the age of 12. Then the doctors left the young couple alone.

The mother did something she had rarely done before: She prayed. She prayed because she was scared and helpless, and praying was all she could do. She believed there was a God, but she had always kept him at a distance. She didn't bother God, and she hoped he wouldn't bother her. She was a good person and even went to church once a year at Christmas, but she had no real interaction or relationship with the Creator.

But now she was at the end of her rope, so she made God a promise: "If you let my baby live, I will give him to you." It was a desperate plea, but it wasn't a hasty bargaining tool. She meant it.

The doctors came in a few hours later. They looked a little confused as they scribbled on their clipboards and whispered to each other. Then one of the doctors cleared his throat and said, "We don't understand it, but your baby is fine. He's totally healthy." The baby was healed totally— it turned out God had some big plans.

I know this story is true because I was the baby. (Gee, you didn't see that coming, did you?) There's a cool lesson in the story of my birth. God puts broken things and broken people back together, physically and spiritually. I was born broken, and God healed me. My mom was spiritually broken, and God healed her. She has lived for Christ ever since that day, and she's one of the most amazing women of God you would ever meet.

≫ Something to Stand On

I know God heals. I am literally living proof. I also know in the Bible it says, "Jesus Christ is the same yesterday and today and forever" (Hebrews 13:8). So everything Jesus did while he was on this planet, he still does. He healed people then—he heals people now. I really don't understand how it works. I just know it does. Jesus was broken so we can be whole. Isaiah says, "He was pierced for our transgressions, he was crushed for our iniquities; the punishment that brought us peace was on him, and by his wounds we are healed" (Isaiah 53:5).

One really good definition for *healing* is "restoration of the original idea or vision." It's like restoring an old painting. Its original beauty is rediscovered.

Let's look at one chunky example. Luke says, "Jesus left the synagogue and went to the home of Simon. Now Simon's mother-in-law was suffering from a high fever, and they asked Jesus to help her. So he bent over her and rebuked the fever, and it left her. She got up at once and began to wait on them. At sunset, the people brought to Jesus all who had various kinds of sickness, and laying his hands on each one, he healed them" (Luke 4:38-40).

Jesus is still healing. He hasn't retired. The promises in the Bible have no expiration dates. But here's a question, and it's a really big question: What about when it seems like God doesn't heal? In the passage we just read, Jesus healed Simon Peter's mother-in-law. That's very inspiring.

But let me tell you about my mother-in-law, Sharon Mortimer. Sharon was the mother of eight kids. My wife,

Diana, is the youngest. Sharon lived in Keokuk, Iowa. Several years ago she was diagnosed with cancer. Her family rallied around her, and she was treated. She started going back to church, and we got some great news. The cancer was gone. Everything seemed good. Sharon and her husband, Jack, celebrated their 50th anniversary. It was a good time.

But a week after the anniversary party, Sharon went to the doctor because she was having stomach pains. It turned out the cancer was back. This time it was in her liver. The family rallied. People all over were praying for her. But she didn't get better—she got worse, and cancer stole her life. What do I do with that? I'm sure many of you wrestle with the same question.

I know our understanding is earthbound and limited. Could it be God has a totally different perspective on healing than ours? His perspective isn't limited by time or space. He views our lives in light of the eternal, not the temporary. Our time on this planet is just a very small part of our lives. The best is truly yet to come—and that's not just some meaningless hype.

I've also talked to people who think when God doesn't heal, it's because people have sinned or have a lack of faith in their life. But I really don't buy that because healing is God's job, not ours, and his love and desire to heal is bigger than our sin or doubt.

I don't know how or why God heals or why he doesn't. I have more questions than answers, but I do know two things.

1. God is good.

God is continually good. It's more than what he does. It's who he is! God can't be not good. It would go against God's nature. He's good, and there's never a time when he isn't trying to bring about good in your life. Bad things happen because we live on a fallen planet held captive by an evil terrorist. We have a very real enemy, Satan, who's doing his best to destroy our dreams and lives.

Sometimes we also make stupid choices, but through it all, God is good. He causes all things to work together for good. He brings good from our pain and heartache. He brings sunshine from our shadows. But sometimes we don't understand how God's working in our lives, which brings us to the second thing I know...

2. God is mysterious.

We won't understand a lot of things on this side of the curtain. We can't figure out God or put him in one of our boxes. We can't prepackage God. God is mysterious—sometimes that's the only answer we get, and it's enough, because without mystery, we wouldn't need faith.

"They all realized they were in a place of holy mystery, that God was at work among them" (Luke 7:16, MSG). The fact that we can't totally figure out God allows us to approach him with a sense of awe and wonder.

God is good; God is mysterious. The two work together. If God were good without being mysterious, he'd be boring. He'd be Mr. Rogers: Safe, sanitized, and predictable—too predictable. If God were mysterious without being good, he'd be creepy and harmful. People have tried desperately to take away God's mystery. They've tried to turn the Creator into a prepackaged formula and to control God. But the problem is, if we take away this mystery, we also take away God's power.

God is mysterious. I know he does (and will continue to do) things I have no explanation for. But because I also know God is good, even in the midst of mystery, I can trust God. That seemed like a pretty good place to start this story.

chapter two

Boy Scout Camp— or My Personal Hell

I was about 12 years old, and for some reason unbeknownst to me, my parents decided I should become a Boy Scout. I think they thought it would be a character-building experience or would make me more of a man or a better American. Instead it...(please pause and read the next statement slowly for dramatic effect) it almost killed me! How's that for hardcore drama?

So I joined the Boy Scouts, and at first, it was actually *almost* fun. We met in the basement of a Methodist church once a week, and we would talk about manly things like football, belching, and how to start a fire using only a twig and a cotton swab. I got the uniform, including the cool neckerchief-bandana thing. Our leader's name was Scoutmaster Dan. He was a gentle, quiet man who looked a little like Abraham Lincoln and smelled a lot like cigarettes. He always wore black dress socks with sandals. I liked being a scout; I was feeling manlier all the time.

But then it happened. I went to—*gasp*—Boy Scout camp! (For further dramatic effect, please let out a blood-curdling scream right now.) It was a week of running around in tick-infested woods, trying to "outman" each other.

The first thing we did when we got there was go to the swimming pool for a swimming test. They wanted to see how many laps we could do so they could classify us for the organized swim time. The more laps you could swim, the deeper you could go in the pool. I lined up; they blew a whistle; I jumped in and started frantically beating the water. Then I sunk like a rock after half a lap. The body-builder lifeguard was laughing, saying, "Look at the girly boy—he can't swim." I pulled myself out of the shallow end of the pool only to be told I would be spending my organized swim time in the kiddie pool. I was just relieved they weren't making me wear floaties.

Then I discovered I had to share a tent with a certified psycho. Alan had been trying to kill me for years. He was the second shortest kid at our school. I, of course, was the shortest. So I was the only one he could get away with picking on. Alan bullied me from kindergarten all the way to eighth grade when he moved away, proving to me there was a God. For nine years he made my life a living heck. He mocked, teased, punched, pushed, tripped, kicked, and humiliated me nonstop. It brought him great joy. Then I went to Boy Scout camp, and they told me I got to share a very small green army tent with the devil-boy—*yippee!* You can imagine my enthusiasm.

We started things off with Alan giving me a major wedgie. I did get him back for this, though. I had only packed one pair of underwear, and he ripped those by pulling them over my head. So I didn't wear underwear the rest of the week. The next time he tried to give me a wedgie, the joke was on him.

Alan put poison ivy in my sleeping bag. He brightened my days with continual verbal abuse. I woke up once, and he was standing over me with a pillow about to suffocate me. (I only wish I were making this up.) After three days he got tired of trying to kill me—I just wouldn't cooperate—so he moved out of our tent.

My new tent mate moved in. His name was Mike. He was a good guy who lived down the street from me. I was excited until I smelled him. Mike had the not-so-bright idea that he could save time and space if he sprayed his clothes down with bug spray before he packed his luggage. It was a very hot and humid summer, so by the time we got to camp, all of his pesticide-saturated clothing had mildewed. He smelled like a dead salmon. It turned out this was the reason he'd gotten kicked out of his last tent. Also, Mike was the camp bugler, so he would get up and practice his trumpet at five a.m. every day.

We spent the week running around the woods, killing and carving things. We ate beef jerky, Vienna sausages, and corn chips. My mom came up on parents' night, and I just looked at her with a scared look on my face and said in a high-pitched whisper, "Help me."

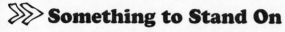

>> Something to Stand On

I obviously survived the week (with minimal emotional scarring), and I learned something. I realized bad times come, but they don't stay. Every bad day, week, month, or year will eventually go away. We all have hard times when we wish we could just stop the world and get off. It might seem like there's no way out of our situation or the tough times will last forever. I've felt that way many times. But as I've gotten older and survived some really harsh things—I have the scars to prove it—I've realized bad days happen, but they eventually go away. No matter what you're facing, you can get through it. Don't give up!

One guy in the Bible went through his own personal "Boy Scout camp" experience. His name was Joseph. His story is found in Genesis 37-50. Joseph had 11 brothers. But he was his father's fave. He was a serious dreamer: He spent most of his time with his head in the clouds. He had a dream his brothers would bow down to him someday. He stupidly shared this dream with his brothers, and they had some serious issues with it. They were jealous and thought he was a snotty little punk.

So they did what any reasonable siblings would do—they sold him...seriously. They sold him into slavery. That could hurt a guy's feelings. He was hauled off to Egypt, where he worked for a guy named Potiphar.

But God was with Joseph, and things went well. Then just when it seemed as if everything was working out, Joseph was thrown into prison because he refused to have sex with his boss' wife. She got mad because he refused her come-ons and accused him of trying to rape her. Joseph had every opportunity to commit adultery if he had wanted to, but he refused to sin against God. He spent years in prison.

Eventually he got out, and God gave him an incredible promotion. He basically became the vice president of Egypt. He was second in command behind Pharaoh. His life drastically changed in one day. He woke up in prison but went to bed in the palace. He was used to save his family and an entire nation.

The designer of your destiny has big plans for you. Your future is bright, *even* when your present really stinks. No matter what you're facing, don't give up. Things will get better. You can make it! Hang in and hang on. Talk to God; talk to someone you trust. Don't give up on yourself.

Boy Scout camp didn't last forever. I lived to tell about it. I even learned some things, and I was much more grateful for certain things, like my home—and restraining orders.

chapter three
Saved by a Wedgie

I'm probably one of the only people on the planet whose life was actually saved by a wedgie. Seriously.

I'm not normally a big fan of wedgies. Over the years I've received hundreds of them, ranging from harmless, wimpy wedgies when my waistband was barely moved to an atomic wedgie at summer camp. One time my underwear was pulled over my head, and I could actually feel my spleen being bruised. I have truly experienced the full gamut of undergarment discomfort. (I'm not necessarily proud of that.) But there was one wedgie I was actually happy to get.

It happened one fateful day when I had gone on vacation with my Uncle Stan and Aunt Diane. We had gone to Six Flags, and on the way home we stopped to swim at a place in southern Oklahoma called Turner Falls. It was a nasty hot summer day. The place was crowded with people looking for a break from the heat. We were having a great time. We were swimming around next to a beautiful waterfall.

Everything was cool, but then suddenly, I hit a drop-off. I was bobbing up and down and flailing around my arms, trying to grab hold of somebody or something. Everybody was just looking at me. I wasn't (and still am not) a great swimmer, so I was drowning.

My life literally passed before my eyes, and I remember thinking, "Wow! This is so sad. I'm going to die without ever growing facial hair." At that point in my young life, my major goal was to grow a mustache, because to my friends, that was the epitome of all that is manly. Note: This goal was finally achieved when I was about 19. I grew a patchy little 'stache. It looked like a greasy caterpillar was hanging onto my upper lip for dear life.

I was sinking like a brick when suddenly I felt my underwear and my cutoff denim shorts being pulled up so forcefully they pulled the rest of my chubby body with them. Uncle Stan had seen me drowning from the beach and, in an amazing display of superhuman speed, had burst from the beach to where I was. I was waving my arms like a wild, scared, little spider monkey, so he couldn't grab me from the front. I would have taken both of us down in my desperation. So he did what he had to do to rescue me. Uncle Stan reached out and grabbed me by the back of my shorts and pulled as hard as he could, and he literally saved my life by giving me a wedgie. It wasn't pretty or comfortable, but it saved me.

>>> Something to Stand On

Since then I've been in many other helpless situations—

physically, spiritually, emotionally, and financially. Times when things were out of my control and I felt like I was a desperate, little spider monkey waving my arms and crying out for help. My Creator has always been there to rescue me. But usually he does it in ways I wouldn't have expected or chosen.

Sometimes when God rescues us, he does it in ways we don't understand. It might be a little uncomfortable. It might even temporarily hurt—like a "soul wedgie." My uncle, in his amazing lifesaving wisdom, knew that if he had tried to grab me from the front or by the arms, I would have pulled us both down. So he came at me from behind and grabbed my shorts. I didn't expect it. I didn't enjoy it. But it was what I needed, and it's what saved me.

When we're going down, God, who is good and mysterious, reaches out and rescues us. And sometimes it's not comfortable, but it's what we need. It's the hurt that brings healing.

Jeremiah 32:17 says, "Ah, sovereign LORD, you have made the heavens and the earth by your great power and outstretched arm. Nothing is too hard for you." When we're in trouble, it's an impossible situation, and God stretches out his arm toward us. What a cool picture! God saves us, and sometimes, it feels a little like a soul wedgie—but it's okay because he is the lifesaver and knows how to save us.

So how do we react? Do we get upset or embarrassed or angry because we don't understand the way God rescues us? I'll tell you what I did in the near-drowning. I was forever grateful. Uncle Stan saved my life by giving me a wedgie.

Saved by a Wedgie

That was a long time ago, and we've spent a lot of time together. Uncle Stan was there when my daughter was born—he was also there when my dad died. We've been through a lot of stuff. I respect him as a great man. I admire the way he has lived his life and treated his family.

Many things have happened since then, but I can't look at my uncle without thinking, *This is the man who once saved my life. Because of what he did, I got to live; I got to meet my wife and daughter; I got to do life with a lot of beautiful people; I got to write this book. I'm forever grateful.* The temporary pain of a wedgie is gone, but the gratitude remains.

It's the same with God. I rarely understand what he's doing in my life, but I can't ever help thinking, *This is the God who saved my life. Because of what he did and what he does, I get to live. I'm forever grateful.*

So What's in a Name?

In biblical times names had incredible significance. They were meant to define who you were or describe something about you or your history. Parents put great thought into naming a child because the name would tag him for the rest of his life. Knowing this, I did a little research hoping to discover something about myself. I discovered what my names mean, and I'm not sure what they reveal about me.

My first name, Luke, means "giver of light and knowledge"—which is cool.

My middle name, Delano, means "picked from the nut tree."

My last name, Lang, means "long or tall"—seriously. Ironic, isn't it?

So I'm a long, tall giver of light and knowledge picked from the nut tree.

So what does your name mean?

chapter four
Jimmy

Jimmy moved next door to me when we were both in either second or third grade. I don't remember exactly when, but I do know we became instant best buddies. He had been held back a year, so he was a year older than me. We would hang out at his house after school and talk about girls, cars, and professional wrestling. We would listen to music and make crank calls. We played football in my front yard. I once crashed his dirt bike into the side of a barn, and he didn't beat me up. That's a real friend.

But like all true friends, we would occasionally get into fights. We'd get all upset and swear we would never talk to each other again ("I hate you, you...you dork-face!"). Then we'd make up the next day ("So you want to ride bikes or what?").

Over the years we became better and better friends, partly because we were totally different. Jimmy was everything I wasn't. For instance—

- Jimmy was cool; I was a hopeless geek.
- Jimmy never did or said anything goofy or stupid.
- Jimmy started shaving when he was about 11. I was in my early 20s.
- Girls liked him—he had actually kissed many real, live girls.

Jimmy was different from me in other ways, too:
- His parents had divorced when he was pretty young. Mine were still together.
- He barely knew his dad—I lived with mine.
- He was forced to grow up pretty fast. I was pretty sheltered.

Jimmy was the one who told me about sex. He even had...um...a visual aid—a JC Penney catalog that had pictures of real, live women wearing nothing but actual undergarments. I know that seems a little sick and lame, but to me it was pretty risqué stuff.

He also tried to teach me how to chew tobacco. It didn't work out well. He gave me a big wad of Red Man chewing tobacco. I put it all in my mouth at the same time and began to gnaw on it. I could feel my stomach rebelling, and my face was progressively getting a deeper shade of green. I puked up several internal organs that day. It wasn't pretty.

Through it all we were buds. We had a great arrangement. Jimmy was my self-appointed bodyguard and defender. I guess because I was a short little goofball, he felt he needed to protect me. I must admit I took advantage of this situation. I'd start fights by being a big mouth, and he would finish them for me. It was a great situation.

Jimmy was one of the first people ever to tell me that I'd grow up and become a minister. He saw something in me and on me that I didn't.

We grew older, high school happened, and we both found our own little groups. We drifted apart a bit. But the foundational friendship was still there.

I moved away and haven't talked to Jimmy in years. Every once in a while, I'll get a report on how he's doing. He's had some hard times. He's been married and divorced a few times, and he's dealt with some huge issues. Life hasn't been kind to Jimmy. But I like to think if we ran into each other, we could pick up where we left off and maybe talk about girls, cars, and professional wrestling—or whatever.

Jimmy

⟫⟫ **Something to Stand On**

It's no accident that friends are such a huge part of our lives. We're wired for relationship. God created us to be friends. He put something inside us that craves friendship. We need each other. Hermits aren't happy people because no one was created to be alone.

The truly amazing part is that God did not only create us for relationship with each other, but he also created us to have a relationship with him. That's right, the Creator of well, everything, wants to have a relationship with us.

It was part of the original Genesis vision. God would come down and take walks with Adam and Eve. Part of the

Freak Factoid

Okay, this really happened. It was my senior awards assembly at Owasso High School. I—along with a handful of my proud classmates—was getting an award for attending the same school system for my entire educational career. It's sad that after 13 years, that is the only thing I had done to deserve an award.

I marched down front to receive my coveted certificate (suitable for framing). I must admit I was wearing a T-shirt about two sizes too small, and because I was a portly fellow, it wasn't good. I looked like a link sausage—or like someone had shoved 12 pounds of Jell-O into a three-pound bag. I was bursting out in all my flabby glory. I was already a little self-conscious about this when, while I was in front of my entire peer group, a guy named Rex shouted out, "LOOK! LUKE IS PREGNANT!"

It was one of those slow-motion moments when it seems like everyone is pointing at you and laughing. Me and my Jell-O made a quick exit. I was a 17-year-old American male, but on the way home from school that day, I cried.

redemption package Christ purchased for us by his death and resurrection is the present reality of a restored relationship with God. We can be friends with God. In fact that should be our primary relationship. If it is, it will trickle down and affect every other relationship in our lives.

When I was younger I wanted to be famous. I wanted to be known. I wanted to have an impressive label like "athlete," "rock star," "VIP," or "celebrity." As I've gotten much older and hopefully a little wiser, I really only care about one label: "Friend of God." It's the only one that matters, and it's the one label we're all meant to wear.

Jimmy

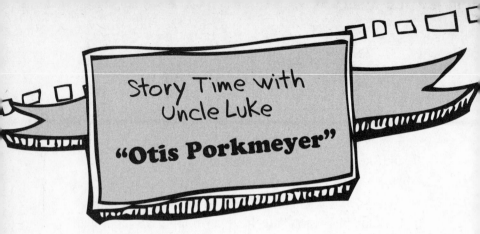

Otis Porkmeyer was the man
who couldn't laugh or smile.
Grumpiness and despair
were Porkmeyer's daily style.

Everybody wondered why.
Did he swallow something sour?
Were his boxers way too tight?
Or he never took a shower?

Did he really dislike fun?
What a party pooper!
What on earth could it be
that put Otis in this stupor?

Somewhere, somehow it must just be
imagination died.
He had forgotten how to dream.
He'd become all dignified.

He once would giggle; he loved to wiggle.
He'd shout and run and play.
But then they said to hush, sit still.
"Don't do that. You must stay!"

They told him one too many times
that he was good for nothing.
He never knew or realized
we're custom-made for something!

They told him he should be concerned
with just reality.
Be practical, conform, and then
avoid unconventionality.

Otis listened to those voices.
He let them all affect his choices.

He believed what the masses said,
and gradually his dreams were dead.

So now he lives with zero hope,
and only leaves his room for soap.
He's learned a life without a dream
is like brussels sprout ice cream.

So, my friend, don't be a Porkmeyer.
Hang with people who encourage and inspire!
Avoid dream killers and hope stealers,
the negative, and sorrow dealers.

Don't use words like *wouldn't, couldn't,*
never, cannot, will not, shouldn't.
Find the ones who spread the good.
Use such words as *would, could, should!*

Remember always to dream and hope
and take much time to play.
Be sure to laugh and wiggle and giggle
a little bit each day!

chapter five
Potty Mouth

Hey, here's a major news flash for you: Sex can make you stupid. Shocking, isn't it?

Oh yes, it's true. You might be a reasonable, intelligent person, but whenever a good-looking guy or girl, whichever the case may be, smiles at you or acts the least bit interested in you, suddenly, you don't know who you are or what you're doing. You're reduced to a blubbering mound of nerves. There's actually a medical term for this sad state. It's called "momentary hormone-induced stupidity."

I first realized the truly stupidifying power of the opposite sex when I was about 12. I was at my cousin Matt's house, and we were riding bikes. I have to tell you my bike was no ordinary bicycle. It was, quite possibly, the coolest bike in the world. It was metallic lime green. (Please keep in mind this was 1977.) It had a banana seat, which was very uncomfortable but looked really cool. It also had curly-fry handlebars—tall, chrome handlebars that twisted around several times. My bike was totally funkadelic.

Because I had the coolest bike in the neighborhood—who are we kidding? in the entire free world—I was feeling pretty good about myself. We were having a great time.

Matt had a dried-up creek behind his house. A little flat wooden bridge ran across the creek. For some stupid reason that was where we decided to ride bikes that day.

Here's where things really started to get ugly. This girl lived across the street from my cousin. She was a serious hottie, even though she didn't have a neck. Okay, technically, she had a neck, but it was a very small neck. So her head looked as if it was just sitting on her shoulders. This didn't bother me; I still thought she was beautiful. Her neckless condition would just hinder me from giving her a hickey, which was okay because at the time I didn't understand how the whole hickey thing worked anyway.

So this girl came over to my cousin's house. I was trying desperately to get her to notice me somehow. I was being loud and popping wheelies on my funkadelic bike. But nothing was working. It was like I was invisible to her. So I decided to take drastic measures. I decided to show her exactly how brave and daring I was.

As I was riding over the bridge, I would ride as close as I could to the edge of the bridge without falling to certain death. I know this sounds pretty pathetic, but to a 12-year-old in rural Oklahoma, this was death-defying, gut-wrenching excitement. I could tell I'd finally gotten her attention. She was digging me—I could tell. She was even smiling and pointing at me.

But then it happened. I got a little too close to the edge of the bridge, and I flew right over the edge. I landed face down on the rocky creek bed. I had mud and blood all over me. I broke my two front teeth. The no-neck hottie laughed at me and called me a clumsy dork. I was humiliated and in pain. My mom rushed me to the dentist.

My dentist, Dr. Daniels, looked and acted like the old comedian Jerry Lewis. He had really hairy hands—this was back before dentists wore rubber gloves—so his hand hair would tickle the roof of my mouth. (Yes, it was pretty gross.) Dr. Daniels put two caps on my front teeth. The caps are made of porcelain, which is the same stuff they use to make toilets. So technically, I'm a true *potty mouth*.

⫸ Something to Stand On

Sadly, this was just the first in a really long list of stupid things I've done to try to impress the opposite sex. In fact almost every dumb mistake I made as a teenager or young adult can be traced to a female. She'd walk into the room, and I'd lose the ability to think or speak clearly.

The reality is, sex can make you crazy. And that complicates life because we're constantly bombarded with sex. A lot of songs, movies, and TV shows are all about sex. We're slammed with magazines and Web sites with sexual images and themes. It can make you nuts.

It's actually very serious stuff. Many people have forfeited their future for momentary pleasure. They cannot only mess up their life but also hurt a lot of people around them.

I got hurt because I was playing too close to the edge. I ended up breaking part of my face, and I was left with a permanent reminder of my own stupidity. Sadly, many of us approach our love lives the same way. We wonder how close we can get to the edge before we fall off. I see this attitude reflected in a question I've been asked many times by teens, adults, and even a few senior citizens.

The question is: "How far can I go?" In other words how far can I take this? What can I get away with before I cross the line? How far can I go before I tick off God? Those are the *wrong* questions.

The question we should be asking is, "How close can I get?" How close can I get, not to the opposite sex, but to the one who should be my first love? How close can I get to Jesus? If that's my primary question and concern, then all of my other relationships will fall into place, and I won't fall over the edge. I won't live a broken life. Instead I'll live a life continually in pursuit of a closer, deeper, fuller relationship with my Creator.

That's what we were made for. The all-knowing, all-powerful higher power desires to have a deep, ongoing, on-growing relationship with us. The Bible says, "Seek first his kingdom and his righteousness, and all these things will be given to you as well" (Matthew 6:33). That's good news for potty mouths like me.

chapter six
Second-String King

➡️ *I'm not athletic. I know we've already pretty much established that, but it's fundamental to this chapter. I have the motor skills of yogurt. So I'm by no means a jock, which is a bummer because I love sports. I'm a hardcore Dallas Cowboys fan. That's right—the Cowboys, the single greatest sports dynasty of all time. I've always wanted to be a jock, but I just don't have the skills.*

The single worst thing about being unathletic was junior high gym class. I used to hate gym class. Even now, many years later, just thinking about it makes me break out in a cold, nervous sweat. I hated changing in front of the other guys. They had muscles and actual body hair. I was two feet shorter than them, and I was built like Jabba the Hut. I had absolutely no body hair.

It was a daily dose of humiliation, just showing up. The P.E. teacher was no help. He was an old jock who was trying to relive his high school glory days. He had perfect hair and perfect teeth, and he pulled his polyester athletic shorts up way too high. If you weren't a jock or a cheerleader, he didn't have time for you.

But the worst part of gym class was picking teams. The P.E. teacher, God bless him, would pick the two most popular and athletic kids in the class to be the captains. They would then proceed to pick the other athletic and popular kids. The whole time I stood there watching everyone else get picked, I tried to act like I didn't care, but I desperately wanted to be picked. I just wanted to be part of a team. I wanted to belong. Everyone else got picked. It would be down to me and the girl with the broken leg. Finally, the P.E. teacher would make them pick me.

Then I would proudly proceed to the bench where I sat for the next 45 minutes. I still have bench marks on my buttocks because of all of the quality time I spent there. But I eventually made it through junior high gym class—without therapy, I might add.

Over the years all my sweaty attempts to be a jock failed miserably. I tried every major sport and embarrassed myself at every one. It hurt because it's something I really wanted. I thought it was my ticket to popularity and self-acceptance. But instead it just brought me more major humiliation.

But something was happening in the midst of the humiliation. As I learned what I couldn't do—basically anything requiring coordination—I also learned what I could do. I could do a lot of things. I could draw; I could make people laugh; for a little fat guy, I'm a pretty good dancer (oh yes, it's true). I chose to dwell on the things I could do.

In time I learned to live with the fact that my face will never be on a Wheaties box. I'll never be anybody's MVP. I'll never have endorsement deals. And that's okay, because I realized I was picked by the ultimate team captain. The Creator and maintainer of the universe picked me! God pointed down through history and said, "I have chosen you. I have called you by name." Nobody made him do it. God did it simply because he loves me. It's not about what skills or abilities I bring to the team. If it were, I'd still be sitting on the bench. It's all about God's love.

And here's some more good news. Not only did God choose me, but he also made it possible for me to be adopted into his family (more about that in chapter 20). So the coach is my heavenly Father, which is cool because guess who always gets to play regardless of how bad she is? The coach's kid. The same God who picked me also picked you. He did it simply because he loves you.

Something to Stand On

In the Bible we see that God also picked a little second-string shepherd boy to be a king. The boy's name was David, and here's some of his story:

> Now the LORD said to Samuel, "You have mourn-
> ed long enough for Saul. I have rejected him

as king of Israel. Now fill your flask with olive oil and go to Bethlehem [later also the site of another King's big debut]. Find a man named Jesse who lives there, for I have selected one of his sons to be my king."

So Samuel did as the LORD instructed him. When he arrived at Bethlehem, the elders of the town came trembling to meet him. "What's wrong?" they asked. "Do you come in peace?"

"Yes," Samuel replied. "I have come to sacrifice to the LORD. Purify yourselves and come with me to the sacrifice." Then Samuel performed the purification rite for Jesse and his sons and invited them to the sacrifice, too.

When they arrived, Samuel took one look at Eliab and thought, "Surely this is the LORD's anointed!" But the LORD said to Samuel, "Don't judge by his appearance or height, for I have rejected him. [Man, I love this Scripture!] The LORD doesn't see things the way you see them. People judge by outward appearance, but the LORD looks at the heart." [Read that again—I really like that part.]

Then Jesse told his son Abinadab to step forward and walk in front of Samuel. But Samuel said, "This is not the one the LORD has chosen." Next Jesse summoned Shimea, but Samuel said, "Neither is this the one the LORD has chosen." In the same way all seven of Jesse's sons

Second-String King

were presented to Samuel. But Samuel said to Jesse, "The LORD has not chosen any of these." Then Samuel asked, "Are these all the sons you have?" "There is still the youngest," Jesse replied. "But he's out in the fields watching the sheep and goats." "Send for him at once," Samuel said. "We will not sit down to eat until he arrives."

So Jesse sent for him. He was dark and handsome, with beautiful eyes. And the LORD said, "This is the one; anoint him." (1 Samuel 16:1, 4-12, NLT)

Here's a quick history lesson: The nation of Israel had demanded a king so they could be like the other nations. It was like geographic peer pressure: All the cool nations had a king. Why couldn't they? God picked a man named Saul to be the first king, but Saul blew it. He repeatedly disobeyed God, and eventually, he lost it all, including his mind—how's that for real-life drama?

So God picked someone else to lead his team. When picking someone, God doesn't look at the same external things we do. He picked a young sheep herder who wasn't on anybody's most likely to succeed list. His own father forgot him and almost left him out of the lineup (that can really hurt a guy). But despite being the last one picked by man, David was picked by his Creator. God had chosen David. He had some really big plans for him.

David realized God had picked him. But that didn't mean things were going to be easy or that all David's problems were over. David had to overcome some major obstacles in his life. He faced some of the same hurdles we face.

David marched to the beat of his own drum. He had some interests and talents that weren't quite the norm. He played the harp—I wonder if they had band camp back then?—and he had some serious slingshot skills, which is cool but a little different. David had skills he would use later in life, but as a teen, they didn't get him invited to any parties. He spent most of his time hanging out with sheep. He would sit and play his harp for his handful of smelly livestock. I'm sorry, but that's a little creepy.

David's family was seriously dysfunctional. Samuel, the spiritual leader of Israel, came to anoint the next king. Jesse went through all of his sons and almost forgot about the youngest who was out on a hill somewhere singing to sheep (again...just a little creepy). David's dad almost left him sitting on the bench.

David knew what it was like to be forgotten, left out, and left behind. David wrote in Psalm 27:10: "Though my father and mother forsake me, the LORD will receive me."

Maybe you can relate. Things have happened to you that were beyond your control. Maybe you've been rejected, forgotten, and left behind. Maybe you feel like you're living an *almost* life. You *almost* succeeded once. You *almost* lived out your dream. You *almost* had it made. But things didn't work out. You came up short, and now you feel like the perpetual runner-up in the pageant of life. You are always Mr. or Miss Congeniality. You need to know God hasn't forgotten you or left you behind.

God has this to say: "For I know the plans I have for you...plans to prosper you and not to harm you, plans to give you hope and a future" (Jeremiah 29:11).

God has picked you, and you need to trust that he has your best interests at heart. You need to allow God to be strong where you are weak. Realize God can use our limitations because they bring him glory. Give God your strengths and your weaknesses.

All through the Old Testament God tells his people, "I will fight for you." You have limitations—we all do. But you aren't alone. Your Creator stands with you, and he stands for you. Trust him.

David also had to overcome the labels others had put on him. Others had branded him with their words as small and insignificant. He had to get past the fear of what others thought of him.

Not too long after Samuel anointed David, the future king, there was a war, and David's big brothers were in the army. David was too young to enlist, but one destiny-determining day, Jesse sent David to take some lunch—maybe some sandwiches, corn chips, and a little camel milk—to his brothers on the battlefield. When David arrived he found his big, tough brothers, along with the rest of the Israelite army, scared out of their brains because of a big bully named Goliath, who was stomping around, making threats, and mocking God. This bothered David, and he wondered out loud why nobody was fighting this big thug who was blaspheming God.

His oldest brother, who was probably still a little ticked he didn't get picked to be the next king, lashed out at David: "When Eliab, David's oldest brother, heard him speaking with the men, he burned with anger at him and asked, 'Why have you come down here? And with whom did you leave those few sheep in the wilderness? I know how conceited you are and how wicked your heart is; you came down only to watch the battle' " (1 Samuel 17:28).

His brother put labels on David: small, insignificant, conceited, wicked, unwanted. David didn't allow his big brother to discourage or distract him. He went out armed with a few rocks and a slingshot and killed the giant. You can read all about this serious beatdown in 1 Samuel 17.

David could have allowed his brother to define him. But instead he decided to let his relationship with God define him. He took God's word for his life instead of misplaced labels or public opinion. In Psalm 139:13-14 David wrote, "For you created my inmost being; you knit me together in my mother's womb. I praise you because I am fearfully and wonderfully made."

What an incredibly beautiful picture. The Creator carefully knitting together the creation. The designer of the universe carefully and deliberately designing the human race. David realized that, and so should you.

What have people labeled you? Worthless, loser, good-for-nothing, a mistake? Well, the Creator and constructor of everything good says you are wonderful. You were created in God's image.

When people label you—and they will because we live in a world that thrives on labels—reject the lies and remember the truth. The truth about who you are, the truth about who God is, and the truth about what he thinks about you.

You've been picked! God has chosen you. Nobody made him do it. God picked you simply because he loves you. He looked down throughout history, pointed at you, and said, "I choose you. I want you. I know you, and I still choose you." You've been picked—get in the game.

A Mindless Poetry Slam with Uncle Luke

Grab your favorite heavily caffeinated beverage—it's time for a little poetry slam.

My sincere apologies if you're a fan of the color beige or if you're currently wearing beige—this isn't intended in any way to be a comment on your taste or fashion sense.

I hate beige!
It's the color of cubicles designed to confine.
It's conformity, giving up, and standing in line.

Man, I hate beige!
It's the color of the flavorless horde
Who live their lives perpetually bored.

Boy, do I hate beige!
It's the color of Monday, sad songs, and tasteless food.
Also the shade of blah, apathy, and a foul mood.

I really, really hate beige.

It's bland, inoffensive, and politically correct.

It's the pale hue of mediocrity, I suspect.

I hate beige!

chapter seven
Training Band?

It was August 1975. I was a classic under-achiever entering the fifth grade. I was determined this would be the year I finally found my place in the middle school social jungle. I desperately wanted to fit in and actually be good at something.

I had the opportunity to try out for the school band. I was so excited. I just knew music was going to be my thing. And besides, it's a universal truth that chicks dig musicians. So I joined the band.

The first thing we had to do was get our parents to buy us an instrument. Everybody else's folks went down to the really impressive-looking music store and bought beautiful, shiny new instruments. But my mom went to a garage sale and found a 32-year-old trumpet. She paid seven bucks for it. It wasn't beautiful, shiny, or new.

The first thing I noticed when I opened the beat-up case was the musty smell. It smelled like a combination of nasty feet, corn chips, and a nursing home. I tried to play it the first time, and foul green goop came out of all the valves. It was 32 years worth of other people's spit. It wasn't a super-pleasant experience.

Needless to say, I didn't feel good about my instrument. I never practiced, which I guess is pretty important, and I really didn't have any musical ability in the first place. So all of these factors combined made me quite possibly the worst student musician in northeast Oklahoma.

I was really bad, so I ended up in the training band. This was the "special" class for people not good enough for the real band. We were supposed to practice all week, which again, I actually rarely did; then on Friday afternoon, we went into a small, stuffy closet office with the band director and tried out. It was like a twisted version of *American Idol*. We would play a simple musical score, and he would tell us if we were good enough for the real band. I was in training band for three long years. Finally, in the eighth grade, the band teacher kicked me out of the training band—pretty sad, huh?

⟫ Something to Stand On

Some of you might feel as if your life has been one long training band. You just never seem quite to measure up. You're always just one step behind. Your life is like a candy bar, and on the wrapper it says, "You might already be a winner." Suddenly, you get a little excited because after all, you might already be a winner. So you carefully tear open the wrapper only to read the words, "Sorry, you are not a winner."

You feel like your entire life is like that candy bar wrapper. You were optimistic at first. You had hope, you had potential. But as your life has unwrapped, nothing has worked out, and you're left with the message, "Sorry, you are not a winner." You feel like a perpetual loser. Maybe you've suffered through a lifetime of losing. If that's the case, I plead with you: Don't give up and don't give in.

If you're reading this, it isn't too late for you. The game isn't over. No matter how old you are and how many times you've failed, no matter what your family situation is, there's still hope for you. The Bible is full of late bloomers. Abraham didn't realize God designed his destiny of being a daddy until he was 100 years old. Moses was 80 when he ran into a burning bush and found out what he was supposed to do with his life. Even Jesus lived at home until he was 30. So regardless of your past, it's never too late for a comeback.

If you feel like your life is a series of losses, maybe it's time to redefine the concept of winning. We can have such a distorted view of winning. We think for someone to win, someone else must lose.

But the Bible makes it clear that true winning isn't about measuring up or beating someone else. The truth is, winning is all about losing (ironic, isn't it?). Jesus gives us a game plan totally contrary to every self-help book on the shelf. In Luke 17:33, he says, "Whoever tries to keep their life will lose it, and whoever loses their life will preserve it." So if you want to win, lose. Go ahead—be a loser.

Training Band?

Lose your—

- Fears
- Hang-ups
- Ambitions
- Plans
- Goals
- Failures
- Successes
- Strengths
- Weaknesses

Lose yourself!

We lose ourselves by giving our lives, ambitions, goals, strengths, and weaknesses to God. We decide we aren't going to live for ourselves any longer. We lose ourselves in the pursuit of knowing and living for something bigger than us. When we do that, something truly awesome happens: God takes our lives and dreams, does an extreme makeover, and gives us bigger, even wilder dreams.

Lose your life in the pursuit of what really matters—the kingdom of God. That's the only real way to win. That's really good news to those of us who have spent time in training band or on the bench or staring at losing candy bar wrappers. Jesus is for losers.

Training Band?

chapter eight

The Single Most Important Thing
I Ever Learned in English Class

➡️ *My eighth-grade English teacher, Mrs. Dunn, taught me something far more valuable than grammar. Our fifth-hour class gave Mrs. Dunn a very hard time. She was about 64 years old and wore big, flowery, polyester dresses that had gone out of style several decades earlier. She had 15-year-old eyeglasses and matted gray hair she put up in a bun, causing the top of her head to look like a big gray Danish pastry. Her body was one big varicose vein.*

So we made fun of her.

She was different from us, she was old, and she smelled like a combination of medicine and mothballs. So we made fun of her constantly. We were mean and totally merciless.

I'm sure she noticed—we weren't exactly sneaky—and I'm sure it bothered her. But she never let it show. She always had an incredible attitude. We were always mean to her, and she was always nice to us. At the end of the year, I asked her to sign my yearbook. She did, and what she wrote revealed her secret to me.

She wrote, "Dear Luke, always remember, you can catch more flies with honey than vinegar! Love, Mrs. Dunn."

At first I didn't understand it at all. I thought it was a little freaky. I mean, who wanted to *catch* flies?! That's not sanitary. Eventually I realized what she meant, and it didn't have anything to do with catching insects. You get a lot further in life by being positive (sweet like honey) than by being negative (bitter like vinegar). Get it?

Mrs. Dunn taught me a huge lesson about the power of attitude. Your attitude can open or close doors. It can win or lose friends. It's powerful stuff. Your perspective can make the most out of bad situations.

This reminds me of an old, corny story I heard somewhere. Once upon a time there was a science experiment done on two little boys. They were both eight years old, but one of the boys was very optimistic—looked for the positive in every situation—while the other boy was very pessimistic—always assumed or looked for the negative. The scientists took the pessimistic boy and put him in a room full of every imaginable toy or game and left him there. Then they took the little optimistic boy and put him alone in a room full of knee-deep horse manure.

After about an hour had passed, the scientists went back to check on the boys. They looked in on the little pessimistic boy with all the toys. He was sitting in the middle of the floor crying. The scientists were shocked. They ran over to him and asked him what was wrong. The little boy shook his little fists and wailed, "It's not fair! All of these toys! I don't know what to play with first! It's just not fair!"

The scientists scratched their heads, scribbled some notes on their clipboards, and went to check on the second little boy. He was happily skipping around the room. He was singing and slinging pony dung all around. The confused scientists stopped him and asked him what he was doing. The boy looked at them, grinned, and said, "With all of this horse manure, there has to be a pony in here somewhere!"

That's what the right attitude does for us. It causes us to continually ask, "Where's the pony?"

>>> Something to Stand On

Life can get pretty ugly. Things can get bad, but we don't have to let situations or circumstances drag us down. We can rise above the mess by having a healthy attitude. Your *attitude* determines your *altitude*. STOP. Read that last sentence again. Not only is it a chunky little truth, but it's also fun to say. It's kind of like Dr. Seuss meets Dr. Phil. In other words your attitude more than your talent or abilities can determine how high and far you go in life.

Believe it or not, the biblical book of Proverbs has something cool to say about attitude: "A cheerful heart is good medicine, but a crushed spirit dries up the bones" (Proverbs 17:22).

A positive attitude can be a healing attitude in a sick world. Our little planet has been infected with a bunch of negative and destructive forces. We see it everywhere. The effects of sin, hatred, and hopelessness are all around us... that's the bad news (pretty uplifting, huh?). But hey—don't lose heart. The good news (actually, great news) is, because of Jesus living *in* and *through* you, with the right attitude you can be an agent of healing and life. According to Proverbs 17:22, your attitude or outlook can be like medicine. When you're cheerful or happy, you're like a walking, talking pain reliever.

I really love this concept because so many people have the misconception that Christians should never have any fun. People in and out of the church think all Christ followers are boring, uptight people who never laugh, smile, or get excited. They just walk around with constipated expressions on their faces.

This big idea is also floating around that you can't be happy and cool at the same time. I mean, come on—cool people are angry and generally unhappy all the time, right? They're serious and spend a lot of time brooding; and if you're happy, they consider you an intellectual and social lightweight.

But the truth is God wants us to enjoy life. It's really okay to be happy. God wants us to—*gasp*—have fun. We need to realize happiness is a choice. It's up to us. We can choose to have a positive attitude even when negative stuff is happening. Your attitude affects everything in your life. You can't choose what happens to you. Sometimes life stinks, but you can choose your attitude toward each situation.

Your attitude potentially can turn your life into a non-stop party: "All the days of the oppressed are wretched, but the cheerful heart has a continual feast" (Proverbs 15:15). What a great promise. Start looking at your life as a continual feast. Look at every day as a blank slate full of potential and promise.

This doesn't mean you have to be perky all the time. In fact I should warn you: If you're perpetually perky, you'll probably cause other people to want to pound you. It also doesn't mean that everything is going to be continually peachy.

Life is a feast, and like with any good feast, there will be dishes you like and dishes you don't. What that means is that you continually trust God to work on your behalf. You automatically expect God to do good stuff to you and through you. Each day becomes an adventure—and it all follows from your attitude. A positive attitude attracts positive things. A negative attitude...well, you get the idea.

God has given each of us full control of how we respond and react. You have control of your attitude. If you let someone or something ruin your day and put you in a bad mood, you're giving them control over your attitude. Bad things happen. But decide that when life throws poop at you, you are going to look for the pony.

It's the first day of school, 'bout to make my big entrance.
But I feel good 'cause I like my pants!

I look so good I'll put classmates in a trance.
I'm sure they'll say, "Where'd you get those pants?"

I'm so much cooler than my cousin Lance.
He only wishes he had these styling pants.

The pretty girl there smiles as she sneaks a glance.
She's starting to laugh, must be digging these pants.

I'm feeling so good I could jump up and dance.
That way everyone could get a look at my pants!

I mean, look at them...

They're orange and purple—
Corduroy plaid?

What? Wait! These don't look like any pants I've ever had!
HEY...WAIT!
THESE
ARE
NOT
MY
PANTS!

They're a little tight;
Trying to move's a real fight!

If I move too fast, I'll give myself a wedgie!
I'm getting nervous, feelin' a little edgy!

Hey...wait a minute...There's a real good chance
That these must be my grandpa's pants!

They smell like him. He smells like medicine and old cheese.
He likes plaid pants that ride high with patchy knees.

Whoa! These are my grandpa's pants—
That's GROSS!
I only hope nobody knows.

I'm wearing Grandpa's pants at school. What a lark.
Guess that's what I get for getting dressed in the dark!

chapter nine

Everybody Was Kung Fu Fighting

➡️ *As you can probably imagine, my teenage years were a rejection-filled nightmare. The ages of 13 and 14 were a particularly ugly phase. During that time my well-intentioned mom and her boss (who, I'm pretty sure, never liked me) would spend hours conspiring on ways to make my life easier.*

My mom's boss, who not only was a pharmacist but also a black belt in karate, was sure martial arts would be my ticket to popularity and success. He convinced my mom that it would be good for my waning self-esteem and that I would learn some much needed self-defense skills—which would come in handy on the mean streets of Tulsa, Oklahoma.

He convinced me I could be the next Chuck Norris and

talked me into taking karate. I shelled out 45 bucks for the uniform, and I actually got a little excited. Maybe this would be my "thing." Maybe, just maybe I could be the next Chuck Norris. Stranger things have happened, right?

I went the first week and met the instructor. He was a slightly overweight, off-duty cop who took himself entirely too seriously. He had an incredibly thick red neck and a flattop hair cut. During the first lesson he took me aside and spent 15 minutes explaining to me how he was probably one of the toughest men I'd ever meet and then proudly demonstrated this by actually showing me eight pressure points on my body. Because of his vast knowledge and skill, he could, by applying the right kind of pressure to these spots, kill me, temporarily paralyze me, or make me lose control of my bodily functions.

This was terrifying stuff for a 14-year-old, especially the bodily function part. I went home scared but also a little hopeful that maybe I could learn this pressure point stuff so I could use it on the next person who made fun of me because I was short. I would simply press a secret spot on his ear and make him wet all over himself. It would be awesome.

The second week we learned some fundamentals guaranteed to turn us into well-tuned, lethal fighting machines. We learned valuable fundamentals like how to tie our karate belts and how to pronounce cool karate words like *sensei* and *dojo*.

The third week the instructor (or *sensei*) informed us that using the fundamentals we'd learned the previous week, we would be free-sparring with each other. This meant we'd actually be fighting someone else in the class. At first I thought this might actually be fun, but then he teamed me up with the only girl in the class. I was supposed to fight her. Not only was she a girl, but she was also younger and smaller than me. I felt a little sorry for this poor, defenseless female. So I thought I'd just take it easy on her—I'd dance around make it look good, but I wouldn't hurt her.

As I was thinking this, the little girl grabbed me by the collar and flipped me over her shoulder. I quickly hopped up and thought I'd better be a little more careful, but I still didn't want to hurt her because I was brought up learning that you never hit a girl.

Suddenly, she grabbed me and flipped me *again*. Some of the guys in the class started to snicker a little bit. This was embarrassing. I decided I didn't care if she was a girl, she was going down. I assumed an offensive posture and started to make my move. She countered by grabbing me and flipping me *again*.

I lay there on my back listening to everybody, including the instructor, laughing at me—it was horrible. I got up, dusted myself off, and walked out of there. I never went back.

Here's what I got from my time studying the martial arts:

1. an even lower sense of self-esteem

2. how to say thank you in Japanese: *arigato*

3. athlete's foot

chapter ten

Blind Date

It was my first date. I was 17 years old, and it happened to be a blind date. I know...I was a pathetic loser, but I was tired of spending Friday nights hanging out with my parents, watching The Dukes of Hazzard. I was desperate; I wanted a woman—any woman. So I allowed one of my friends to fix me up with a girl who he said would be just perfect for me. He insisted she had a great personality.

I was scared, but I thought, *Hey, this is my friend, my buddy, mi amigo. He wouldn't hook me up with a bad date.* (Boy, was I wrong.) I finally got up my nerve and called her up to ask her out. She sounded nice, even kind of cute; maybe this wasn't such a bad idea.

I grew up in Oklahoma, and I'd heard this girl was a

serious redneck woman, so I planned the date. I thought it would be cool if we went to a rodeo—yeehaw! I got front-row seats because I thought rodeos were like concerts where you wanted to be right up front. Not true—but more on this later.

Finally, the magic evening arrived. I picked her up in my enchanted magic chariot, which was actually a '74 baby blue Ford Pinto. I was pleasantly surprised. I really expected her to look like a Russian professional wrestler, but she was kinda cute. Maybe this was going to be fun after all. She was about one foot taller than me, so it looked as if I was walking around with my mom all night. So that was a little weird, but I was willing to overlook it (or I guess it would be "underlook"?).

She got in the car and we took off. She started talking, and I noticed every other word was a curse word. This girl was a very creative cusser. She would make most Marines blush. Then she leaned over to me and whispered, "Do you mind if I smoke?" I wanted to say, "No, of course not. Do you mind if I vomit in your lap?" Finally, we got to the rodeo where I made two more wonderful discoveries:

Wonderful Discovery #1: My blind date was allergic to horses. So a rodeo wasn't the greatest idea. Her head swelled up, and her nose started running like a faucet. Her face was totally covered in snot. She looked like a glazed doughnut with ears.

Wonderful Discovery #2: It's really not a good idea to sit in the front row at a rodeo. Seriously, take my word on this. Every time a horse or cow runs by, they fling...

ummm...stuff at you. You know, cow stuff. So we ended up with a lap full of manure. (I know we talked about horse manure in chapter eight, but I promise it's just a coincidence, not some weird theme.)

So near the end of my first date, I looked over at this foul-mouthed girl with nasty cigarette breath who was covered in snot and cow manure, and I thought to myself, *She's really not that cute.*

>>> Something to Stand On

This story reminds me of a Bible verse: "Like a gold ring in a pig's snout is a beautiful woman who shows no discretion" (Proverbs 11:22).

Whoa! What a pretty picture. Discretion is like wisdom in action. It's knowing the right thing to do and actually doing it. All around you can see people who are living without discretion. They choose to do whatever they want, and they don't care about right, wrong, or who they hurt. Their lives end up looking like a total train wreck.

A lot of people have head-knowledge but not discretion. They know the facts, but they haven't applied them to their lives. They know what's right and wrong, but they don't do it. It's not enough to know—we also need to do. That's what discretion is. It's putting wisdom, or head-knowledge, into action.

We need to realize discretion can help us. Proverbs also tells us, "Discretion will protect you, and understanding will guard you" (Proverbs 2:11).

And discretion is like a life preserver—it keeps us afloat: "Discretion is a life-giving fountain to those who possess it, but discipline is wasted on fools" (Proverbs 16:22, NLT). If we exercise discretion, it will keep us from hurting ourselves and others. It will give us life and a better quality of life.

So how do we practice discretion? For starters we need to live for tomorrow, not for today. Many people only live for right now, with no thoughts about consequences or their futures. They're only interested in living for the moment and satisfying their every urge and appetite right now. I've seen a lot of people throw away promising futures for a few moments of pleasure.

When I was growing up, I went to summer camp every year. Every time, it seemed like the speaker told a similar story. It always involved either an honor student or star athlete, a teenager with a very promising future. But the teen had one brief moment of indiscretion. She got drunk or used drugs for the first time. Then she went out and was involved in a horrible accident, usually involving a train wreck or a tractor running over someone's head.

That always made me wonder, "Who couldn't outrun a tractor even if she *were* stoned?" The stories always seemed to be designed to manipulate and scare people into making good decisions. But I did learn a powerful, true lesson from the stories. A lot of people have destroyed their dreams because they didn't have discretion. Practicing discretion helps your dreams come true. It's an investment in your future.

Remember: Every choice you make now affects your future. Your life is choice-driven. Your choices determine where you'll go in life. People who realize that live with discretion. Discretion is a solid investment in your future. If you exercise discretion, it will help you live without regrets and avoid compromise so that you can eventually die with no regrets.

Another simple way to exercise discretion is to think before you act or speak. With discretion you think about consequences before you get mad or demand your rights. Discretion actually puts others first. We realize the world doesn't revolve around us. It's wise to invest our lives in the lives of those around us.

One last good reason to use discretion is that it can actually make you better looking. Just like someone who doesn't practice discretion doesn't look quite so good (remember my blind date?), so someone who has discretion looks a bit better. It's not a cosmetic thing. It's a character thing. Character always works its way out, and people with discretion get better and better looking. In other words what's on the inside always finds its way out.

This works both ways. I've seen average-looking people get better looking because of their character and discretion. I've seen good-looking people get really ugly because of what was in their hearts. I've seen people who, because of their choices, have totally changed their appearance.

I recently saw a picture of a girl I went to high school with. Even though we're the same age, she looked about 20 years older than me. Her face looked like a piece of cheap luggage (leathery and splotchy brown) because she has smoked since she was 15. I also know people who now look like toothless refugees because of the chemicals they've put in their bodies. Others have lived for years with regret and shame over stupid choices, and it has totally affected their appearance. They look hard and vacant.

So practice discretion—it's good for you. Discretion directs destiny. Hey—go ahead—get discreet.

chapter eleven

The Return of Potty Mouth

Way back in chapter five, I 'fessed up to the ugly fact that I'm a potty mouth. Go ahead—flip back and reread it. Okay, as I was saying, you learned how I broke my teeth and became the proud owner of two fake teeth. Sadly, the whole tooth story didn't end there. Since that fateful day I've lived with a potty mouth. It's not pretty, but it's true.

Many years later my wife and I were at a women's retreat.

(Important note: Perhaps this would be a good place to explain why I, a proud American *man*, was at a *women's* retreat. It wasn't for anything weird. It was my job. We worked for the district office of our church, and a big part of our job was working with the camping program, which included the women's retreat. So once a year I would spend a weekend with 350 women in West Texas. I was the token male. I was there for heavy lifting and toilet plunging—very glamorous work.)

For about a week before the retreat, I'd been noticing a really nasty taste in my mouth. It tasted like old milk. After a few days a foul stench was also coming from my mouth. I'd try to kiss my wife, and she'd recoil and say, "Eeww, GROSS!"—which isn't the reaction I was going for. Unbeknownst to me one of my caps was coming loose. The concrete used to hold it in place was worn-out. The taste and odor were the result of the rotten tooth and concrete under the cap oozing out.

The tooth finally broke loose at the women's retreat. Diana and I had just gone to bed, and suddenly, I sneezed. Then I felt something come loose and fly out of my mouth. I screamed, "Ohp mypth goshpf! Ipth losteth ah toopth!" (Translation: "Oh, my gosh! I've lost a tooth!") I was crawling around on the floor, looking for my cap. Diana turned on the light, screamed, started giggling uncontrollably, and turned off the light.

Something rotten had been exposed—the ugly, little, gnarly, broken tooth underneath my cap. It wasn't even a tooth anymore, just a little rotten nub. Without my cap I looked like a mutant hillbilly. My wife couldn't look at me without throwing up in her mouth a little. Also *not* the reaction I want from my loving spouse.

>>> Something to Stand On

I got my tooth nub recapped. But it made me think about how often we try to cover up the ugly things in our lives. But eventually, we have to confront those things. They get exposed. And then we're forced to get honest with God, ourselves, and others.

It's better to "uncap" those things in our life now. It's better to come clean about our sins and shortcomings instead of waiting till they get exposed. Our futile attempts to cap the ugly things in our lives never work. Those ugly things always get uncovered, and our sins and stink get exposed. The *only* solution is to allow Christ to remove our ugliness with his sacrifice on the cross.

I still live with a potty mouth. My two front teeth are still porcelain. I know there's a very good chance that someday, somehow, at the worst possible moment, one of my caps might come out, and my ugly little rotten nub will be exposed *again*. I'll deal with it.

But more important, I know because of my choice to follow Christ, the ugliness in my life and heart won't be exposed. It's already been extinguished and dealt with for good. That's more good news for a "potty mouth" like me.

chapter twelve

The Peach Cobbler Story

> **Warning—this tale is not for the faint of heart (or stomach).**

Our lives are choice driven. Every choice we make now determines our future. We also need to realize that our choices affect others, even the small choices. This is a scary little story of a time when I had a choice to make.

It all started on a blustery Sunday afternoon. I was going out to eat with my pastor and his family. I wasn't feeling well at the time. I was just getting over a bad cold, but I was a 19-year-old junior college student, so I never turned down a meal. We went to this family-style restaurant where everybody sat at a big round table together. The staff brought out incredibly large portions of greasy comfort food, and you just served yourself—it was a wonderful thing.

We sat there and ate and ate and ate, and then when we were almost through, they brought us dessert. Dessert was a big, beautiful, hot peach cobbler. So we ate it, too—

at least we ate most of it. There was a tiny sliver of cobbler left. We were basically finished with the lunch. The waitress had already brought the ticket. We were ready to leave, but then something terrible happened.

Remember, I was just getting over a bad cold. So as we were sitting there, I coughed—I couldn't help it. It was one of those involuntary, violent coughing fits. And when I coughed, something deep inside me dislodged and came flying out of my mouth. Yep, it was a quarter-pound, green lugie.

What happened then almost seemed to be in slow motion. I watched as my lung cookie gracefully flew through the air. It twisted around and around until it finally came to rest right on the top of the last remaining slice of peach cobbler—*gasp!* The strange thing is, most really good peach cobbler has a topping that's a little gooey and moist. So my snot automatically blended right in and looked like part of the topping. I quickly looked around and realized everybody was deep in conversation, and no one else had seen what had just happened. (Whew.)

Right then and there I had a choice to make. I could say, "Excuse me, nobody touch that cobbler because my phlegm is all over it. If you eat it, you'll probably get ill." That would've been the polite thing to do, but I didn't want anybody to think I was the kind of person who goes around coughing on cobbler. That's not socially acceptable. If people think you're a cobbler cougher, they stop asking you to go out to eat with them (and they sure won't pay for the meal). So I didn't say anything, and besides, I rationalized, we were almost done, and nobody was going to eat that little measly piece of cobbler.

The Peach Cobbler Story

So I just sat there choosing to say nothing. But suddenly, to my horror, the plot thickened because my pastor reached over and scooped up the last remaining sliver of cobbler, including my lugie, and put it on his plate—*oh nooooooooo!* I sat mortified in my seat. This was a moral dilemma I wasn't equipped to deal with. Would I allow my pastor, my spiritual leader, to unknowingly eat my snot? I watched as he loaded the defiled dessert onto his fork and lifted it up to his mouth...

Our life is choice driven, and all of our choices have consequences. Our choices, even the seemingly small ones, can affect other people. Sometimes our choices can be a little fuzzy, unlike my cobbler dilemma. That one was crystal clear. I had a choice to make. I could do the right thing at the risk of personal social shame and say, "Excuse me, Pastor, don't eat that cobbler because it's covered in my personal phlegm." Or I could do the wrong thing and just watch as he ate my snot. I had a choice to make—and I made the wrong choice.

≫ Something to Stand On

Okay, I'll give you a minute to collect yourself after that truly disgusting revelation. But seriously, life is all about choices. You'll face many choices in life. Some will be really *big* choices, like who you'll date and marry, whether you will even want to date or marry, what to do with your life. Some will be not-so-big choices, like what you'll wear today, whether or not you want fries with that, paper or plastic.

As Christians we spend a lot of time talking about and trying to figure out what God's will is for us. What on earth does God want us to do? We bring God into the discussion and try to make choices according to what we think he wants. The problem is, a lot of time God's will isn't as clear or simple as we wish it was. We want *all* the answers *right now*. We want God's will to be like MapQuest where we get all the precise directions we need: "At the age of 17½, you will enroll in a small liberal arts college in Kansas..."

But God's will is much more like a fungus—it grows on you a little more each day. It's an organic thing. As you get into God's Word, the Bible, you discover what's important to God. Then you need to decide to live according to those things. You do what you feel God wants you to do today, and then tomorrow you wake up and do the same.

I'll give you a couple of guiding principles, though. God's will for you always involves two things:

1. Your passion

2. God's purpose

It involves your passion. God has already equipped you to do what he wants you to do. What are you good at? What do you enjoy? What makes you smile? Believe it or not, God wired you. He gave you certain abilities and likes. A common misconception is that God will make us do something we hate. It's not true. God wants us to use what we have or enjoy for him. God has given you gifts and passion. But it's your job to take the time to develop those gifts and passions. You need to do all you can to be the best possible you.

The Peach Cobbler Story

I've seen a lot of immensely talented people do nothing because they're waiting for God to somehow dump their destinies in their laps. Don't wait for something magical to happen. Use your gifts now. Take time to define and develop your gifts. It's a pretty sweet partnership: God gives us amazing potential, but we need to do what we can—work, study, practice, train, etc.—to reach our potential. It probably won't be easy, but it will be worth it.

God's will also involves God's purpose. His purpose isn't complicated. We get a picture of God's purpose in Luke 19:10, where Jesus tells us, "The Son of Man came to seek and to save what was lost." That is God's unchanging purpose: to rescue and restore the human race.

You find God's will at the place where your passion intersects with his purpose. It all starts with a choice. When you choose to use your talents and desires to help achieve God's purpose, everything gets set in motion. But it's a daily choice. And you probably won't get all the directions you want. It's *deciding* (cool word) daily to live for God and use your passion for God's purpose.

Now I'm a little hungry—does anybody want some peach cobbler?

Freak Factoid

Okay, this really happened. I was walking through the hall of my daughter's elementary school. Two little boys were behind me. I overheard their conversation, which went exactly like this (I promise):

BOY #1: "WHOA! Is that guy a midget?"

BOY #2: "No, dude, I think he's a fifth-grader."

The Peach Cobbler Story

chapter thirteen

Chasing Jupiter

My daughter was in third grade, and I was dropping her off at school. It was a chaotic scene every morning at 7:40 as hundreds of elementary school students scurried for their classes. The parking lot was like a big scary slow-motion traffic jam as irate and impatient parents competed for the primo parking places.

I was waiting in line to drop Delanie off when I looked over and saw a little girl proudly carrying her science fair project to class. She had made an almost exact replica of the solar system with Styrofoam balls and wire. It's like some kind of unwritten science fair rule that someone has to make either a Styrofoam galaxy or a papier-mâché volcano spewing something that looks like reddish-orange baby food.

This girl's project had a big yellow Styrofoam ball in the middle. This, of course, was the sun. Carefully attached to the sun were multicolored Styrofoam planets of varying sizes. I was impressed. This was a great-looking solar system. She'd done a really good job—okay, in all actuality her parents had probably done a good job but maybe she helped a little.

She was grasping her little universe, trying to carefully maneuver it so no planets got thrown out of orbit. She was just trying to get her interplanetary piece of art to her classroom in one piece. But suddenly a big gust of wind blew her planets apart. They went everywhere. She was chasing little Styrofoam balls all over the sidewalk. I feel a little guilty for admitting this, but I actually laughed at all of this. (I know, I'm a cruel, heartless dirtbag.)

Her universe was suddenly out of her control. Her world went crashing down, and she was left chasing Jupiter. She was scampering around, trying to collect her universe all by herself. Plenty of people standing around could've helped her, but they didn't. There were a bunch of other kids, spiffy-looking crossing guards, and even a few adults. I was just a few feet away from her myself. Of course, I was laughing too hard to be any help. No one helped her until a well-dressed man ran to her, reassured her, and helped her put her galaxy back together. He was her dad.

≫ Something to Stand On

Many times my life has resembled this solar system scenario. I have everything under control; all of my planets are aligned. Then something suddenly happens, and my whole galaxy is blown away.

Maybe you can relate. It feels like you're chasing your world down the sidewalk. The cause could be a heartache, loss, disappointment, or setback. It could be the death of a dream. It could be the betrayal of a friend or the attack of a stranger. People hurt us, things happen, and our world can spin wildly out of control.

When this happens you can make it if you put your trust and confidence in the right place. Proverbs 3:25-26 says, "Have no fear of sudden disaster or of the ruin that overtakes the wicked, for the LORD will be at your side and will keep your foot from being snared." In other words God runs to your aid, reassures you, and helps you put your universe back together.

This world, in its present condition, is a pretty unstable place. Things are constantly changing. (Isn't the phrase "constant change" a great oxymoron?) Things we thought we could depend on can come crashing down all around us. This can leave you feeling pretty unstable and insecure. It's like trying to build a home on sinking sand.

But the truth is, God is able to stabilize our lives. He's constantly constant—God is totally secure and unchanging. When we put our trust in him, we find a solid foundation to help us put our universe back together. He helps us pick up the pieces and works with us so that things will eventually make sense again. So don't chase Jupiter—chase the One who holds the universe in his hand.

chapter fourteen
Squirrels and Ducks, Oh My!

Near the home we had in Dallas was a lovely little man-made pond. It actually was a pretty cool little slice of nature right in the middle of the urban jungle. The pond had some fish, turtles, and a whole community of ducks. At this little neighborhood pond, I learned a huge lesson.

I was driving by the pond one day, and something caught my eye: a nervous little squirrel. He was trying to get from one side of the road to the other. (So...why *did* the squirrel cross the road?) I slowed down a bit to see if this furry little guy could make it across the busy intersection.

He was frantically dodging cars. It was like a spastic squirrel version of the old arcade game *Frogger*. He would barely miss one car and make a mad run for the next piece of safe pavement. I was cheering for him to make it as he made a final sprint for freedom when his little squirrel dreams were crushed by a fast-moving black SUV. Yes, sadly, the poor little guy didn't quite make it. He became just another roadkill statistic. Let's take a moment of silence to remember this ill-fated, little squirrel....

Ahem, okay.

I had almost forgotten about the squirrel incident, when a few days later, I came to the exact same intersection. I was late for work, so I was rushing down the road. I saw brake lights and noticed that several cars were stopped in front of me. I was ticked because I really didn't have time for this, and why were we stopping anyway!?

I finally got close enough to see what the holdup was—a family of ducks crossing the street. It seemed as if they were moving in slow motion. Then one of the ducks stopped and started cleaning herself right there in the middle of the road. We sat there for five minutes. We were all honking and yelling at the duck. One guy even got out of his car and tried to shoo the duck out of the way. But she ignored us all, and finally, when she was ready, she moved to the other side of the road with her family.

As I drove the rest of the way to work, I thought about the squirrel and the duck and the difference between the two. The big difference was a big sign next to the pond. It was a reflective, yellow, triangular sign with the silhouettes of a mama duck and two baby ducks. This was a designated duck crossing. A way had been made for the ducks to safely cross the road—and they knew it. They were protected by an outside source. They could take their time, and nobody could touch them.

But there was no sign or squirrel crossing for my little furry friend. He was totally on his own—and he knew it. He had no protection and therefore no future.

⟫⟫ Something to Stand On

I realized that many times in my life I've felt like the spastic little squirrel. I frantically run from one situation or problem to the next. But it doesn't have to be like that. As a Christ-follower I'm promised protection from an outside source. I know God has made a way for me.

I can be confident and trust God. No matter what danger is zooming around me, I can know he's made it pos-

Freak Factoid

Again, this really happened. Diana and I were leaving a restaurant. We had just enjoyed a great meal, and it was a beautiful night. As we were walking out of the restaurant and onto the sidewalk, an all-American family was walking into the restaurant: a mom and a dad and their two well-dressed kids.

I'm guessing their son was about five or six years old. The little boy looked at me, and then he doubled up his chubby little fist and punched me as hard as he could in the stomach. I must admit, he hit pretty hard for a little kid. It hurt! And I had no idea why this little demon-child I'd never seen before in my life would hit me.

His parents were mortified. My wife was laughing so hard she was about to cry (thanks, Hon). I was doubled over—not because I'm a wimp, but for a five-year-old, the little punk had a killer right hook. I looked up to see the boy glaring at me as if he'd have killed me with his bare hands if his parents would've let him.

I still have no clue what I did to provoke this beating. I guess I just have a way with kids.

sible for me to cross over to the other side. The times I feel boxed in, when it seems like there's no way out, I just need to act like a duck instead of a squirrel. I can move in the knowledge that God has prepared a way for me to make it. I don't have to be afraid or nervous.

Sometimes life moves fast and furiously. I don't always know which way to go—okay, I *usually* don't know which way to go. But a power higher than me has made a way. It's almost like the Holy Spirit is our personal crossing guard (without the ugly orange vest). So whenever you choose to operate according to God's traffic laws—which he's revealed in his driver's manual, the Bible—you can rest assured that whatever road in life you find yourself trying to get across, a way has been made. You have protection. So go ahead...step out.

Squirrels and Ducks, Oh My!

Norbert has a big proboscis.
A huge, ginormous nose!
And, oh, its appearance is just plain weird
Like a crossed mango and garden hose!

People stare and then look away,
Hoping he doesn't notice, I suppose.
But the actual factual is—it's true—
That Norbert knows his nose!

He knows his schnoz is just plain big
And shaped like tropical fruit.
But it's okay. In fact, you see,
He actually likes his snoot!

He smiles because
He thinks it's real funny,
Especially when
It's red and runny.

That's just the start. All Norbert's parts
Will often make him giggle.
He laughs a lot when he chews food
'Cause it makes his ears both wiggle.

He snorts out loud at his little toes
'Cause they're shaped just like cheese curls.
Just mention his neck or belly button,
And he'll laugh until he hurls.

Norbert wouldn't change if he could.
He's totally self-content.
Norbert likes all of the things
That make him different.

Norbert knows the truth, you see.
Even though we have same parts,
We're different sizes, shapes, and colors
With varying degrees of smarts!

Our differences are what make us unique.
So Norbert celebrates his hairy, huge feet.
Our differences make us one of a kind.
Everyone's a limited-edition, priceless find!

Story Time with Uncle Luke: "Norbert Knows His Nose"

If you try with all your time
To be like Jane or Bill,
There'd be an empty spot in history
That only you could fill.

You are not like anyone else
In all the whole wide world.
So don't you go and follow the crowd.
Let the real you be unfurled!

chapter fifteen
Black and Blue Angels

We were driving from Florida to Texas. It was 12:30 a.m. on July 10, which also happens to be Diana's birthday. We were on our way home from a summer camp. We were driving through Pensacola, and it was becoming increasingly evident by the types of businesses and buildings we were surrounded by that we were on the wrong side of the tracks. But we were tired and desperate.

We'd been driving for hours looking for a place to spend the night. There were four of us in our little Honda: Diana, Delanie, one of Delanie's friends, and me. The two girls were sound asleep in the backseat. Diana and I were cranky (hard to believe, but true). We really just needed a place to stay, but there was no room at the inn—or the

Motel 6 or any of the other seemingly hundreds of hotels and motels we had stopped at.

It turns out that, unbeknownst to us, we were traveling during Blue Angels weekend, which is a really big deal in western Florida. The Blue Angels are a super-elite division of the Air Force. They do death-defying tricks and spins in jet planes. During this particular weekend in July, they do a huge, impressive air show extravaganza. It's evidently big stuff. People come from all over to see it.

These people had taken every available hotel and motel room in this part of the state. We had been stopping at every exit for five hours and at each place were told we weren't welcome. We weren't feeling the love from Florida at this point.

We were desperate, so we pulled into a dimly lit motel parking lot. The motel was really run-down and seedy looking. We parked, and I was about to run into the office to try to get a room when Diana had a funny feeling about the place. Because I'm a wise man, I've learned to trust my wife's funny feelings—we later found out the motel was a front for prostitution and drugs, not the kind of place we wanted to take two 10-year-old girls. So we left the shady motel.

As we were pulling out of the parking lot, we were hit by a lady in a beat-up El Camino. She didn't have her lights on, so we pulled right in front of her. There's no uglier sound than crunching metal in a car crash. She hit us hard—we spun around, and everything was flying around the car—including the big 72-ounce drinks we had bought earlier. One spilled all over Diana. As she reached up and felt her face, she was sure she was bleeding. She wasn't; she was just covered in Pepsi.

Miraculously, we were all fine. The girls had slept through the whole adventure. The lady in the El Camino seemed to be fine, too, at first. She ran over to check on us. She was talking to us until the police arrived, and then suddenly, she fell to the ground and started screaming and flopping around like a fish. The ambulance came and took her away.

The cops took notes and quickly cleaned up the crash scene. They gave us a ticket, but they were nice enough to call local hotels and tell us we were definitely out of luck. There were no rooms available anywhere. Then... they *left*—leaving us stranded in the middle of the 'hood at 1 a.m. with nowhere to go and no way to get anywhere (thank you, Pensacola Police Department).

We ran across the street to a convenience store to call a tow truck. Then it really struck us—we were deserted in a very bad neighborhood. This wasn't good. Even though it was 1 a.m., the convenience store was very busy. We were surrounded by people who didn't want us there. As we made phone calls, we were approached by several angry people who asked us for money. It was scary.

That's when *he* showed up.

I was standing there, trying to look tough. I was doing my best Chuck Norris imitation, but no matter how hard I try, I'm still a five-foot-tall cheeseball, so I don't look really mean. I turned around to say something to Diana, when suddenly, a very large, very tough-looking, bald, black man was standing there. He seemed to appear out of thin air: One second he wasn't there; the next second he was. He was wearing a muscle shirt and built like a professional wrestler. He literally towered above me, and I looked into his face. I noticed he had very gentle, friendly eyes. I also noticed at that moment I didn't feel any fear—I actually had a very peaceful feeling.

He looked at me and said, "You've had a wreck, and you have no place to go. Don't worry. I won't leave you until you have a place to stay." I looked at him and said, "Umm...okay."

Because 10-year-old girls have bladders the size of cashews, just then I had to take the girls into the store to use the restroom. I was hesitant to do this because Diana was on the phone with the insurance company. I really didn't want to leave her, but our new large friend reassured me he'd take care of her. Then he positioned himself between Diana and everyone else with his arms crossed in a bodyguard pose.

The tow truck finally came and hitched up our broken Honda. Our new large friend told me, "Tell the driver to take you to such-and-such hotel; they'll have a room for you." I said, "Dude, you're like an angel." (And yes, I did feel a little weird saying that to a large, mysterious man.) He just kind of chuckled and winked at me. I hopped up in the tow truck and turned around to thank him, but he'd disappeared. There was no place for him to go, but he'd vanished.

The half-asleep, redneck tow truck driver took us to the hotel our new friend had recommended. They had *one* room that had become available a few minutes before we got there because of a cancellation. We got the only available room in town. Cool, huh?

We did, eventually, safely make it home. I have no doubt we had some help, some serious supernatural help. I don't think the Blue Angels were the only angels in town that weekend. I'm convinced that on a humid night in Pensacola, we were allowed a glimpse into the invisible realm and met a large, tough-looking black angel.

chapter sixteen
A Rambling Conversation with Myself

 Note: *Somewhere deep inside my psyche, I ran into my 13-year-old self. We had a little talk. Here's the official transcript.*

OM = Old Me
TYOM = 13-Year-Old Me

OM: Hey! I recognize you.

TYOM: Do I know you?

OM: Actually, you are me. Or rather in a few decades, you will be me.

TYOM: Whoa! This is really weird. I don't know what to say.

OM: You sound a little disappointed?

TYOM: It's just—I was hoping I would look a little more like Barry Gibb. (Cultural side note: For those of you born after 1980, Barry Gibb was part of the extremely cool supergroup The Bee Gees. The man was a master of feathered facial hair, and he knew how to rock a white leisure suit and big gold chain. I'm not ashamed to admit that when I was 13, he was my fashion role model.)

OM: Sorry, this is as good as it gets.

TYOM: That's okay. Actually, you don't look or seem that different from me.

OM: Yeah, my taste in clothing, music, food, and humor hasn't really changed in 30 years.

TYOM: That's a little disturbing. Well, since I ran into you, I do have a very important question.

OM: Go ahead.

TYOM: Will I ever kiss a girl?

OM: You mean besides the really messed-up attempt at spin the bottle last year?

TYOM: Yeah, I'm trying to forget about that.

OM: The first girl you kiss will be your wife, and you won't kiss her until you're engaged. Hey, I couldn't help but notice you have something on your shirt.

TYOM: Yeah, I just got thrown into the dumpster outside the cafeteria again.

OM: Oh, man. Sloppy Joe day?

TYOM: Yeah. I hate my life!

OM: About that—there's something I need to tell you. I know you pretty much hate everything about yourself right now. You hate the way you look and act. You hate the fact you don't fit in anywhere, and it seems like nobody understands you. I know you go home and cry every night and pour out your heart to your Irish setter.

You need to know—despite what a few socially confused people have told you, these aren't "the best years of your life." Things are going to get better—much better. Right now you can't see past the pain, but please hang in there. Someday you'll make sense. God really does love you more than you can image.

TYOM: Ummm...okay. Any last words of advice?

OM: Yeah, be nice to Dad. It turns out he won't be around forever.

TYOM: Anything else?

OM: Yeah, in a few years, somebody is going to suggest you get a perm—don't do it. You'll save yourself the embarrassment of walking around for months looking like a French poodle is glued to your head.

TYOM: Well, thanks, this has been enlightening.

OM: Don't mention it. Hang in there. I'll see you in about 30 years.

chapter seventeen

Allow Me to Rant

Here's a random list, in no particular order, of things I hate. Okay, I know hate is such a strong word, and I know it's not very politically correct, but I strongly dislike these things, so here goes.

I hate:

- Liver
- Mosquitoes
- Hypocrisy
- Urinals (Remember, I'm 5'1"—urinals are not designed for people my height. Most of them come up to my chest...not cool or sanitary.)
- Eye boogers
- Arrogance (especially spiritual arrogance)
- Narrow-minded attitudes toward music or art

- Blue corn chips (seem a little unnatural to me)
- Dress shoes
- Cilantro
- Nose hair
- Protocol and politics
- Decaffeinated coffee (What's the point?)
- Bikini briefs (Again, what's the point?)
- Conformity
- Cats (There, I said it—I feel better.)
- Asparagus
- The day after Christmas
- Cheap toilet paper
- Good-byes
- Monday mornings
- Dream killers
- The word *duh*
- Pain
- Greed
- Polyester
- Heat rash
- The Devil and the way he tries to hurt people and mess up their lives

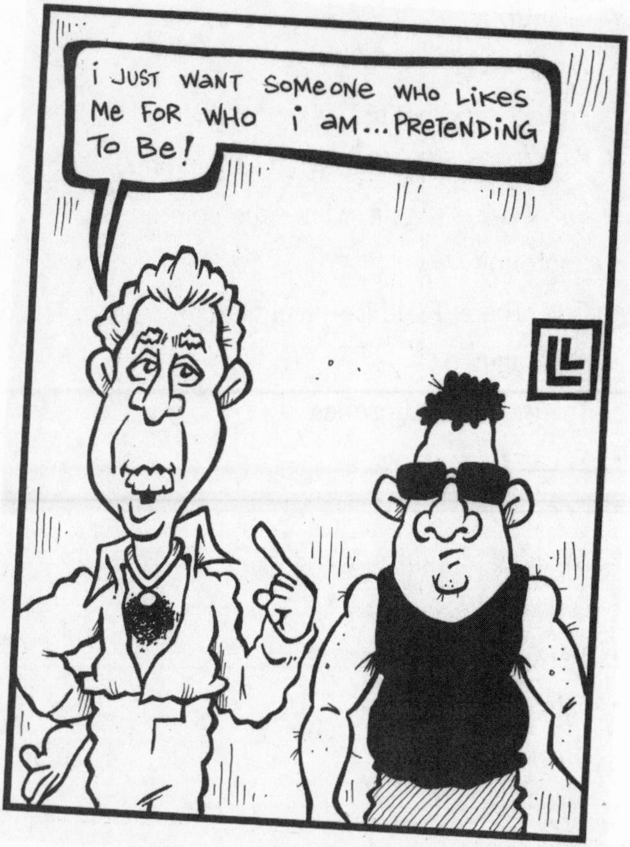
i JUST WANT SOMEONE WHO LIKES ME FOR WHO i AM... PRETENDING TO BE!

chapter eighteen
Soiling Myself Shogun Style

Diana and I were enjoying a nice, quiet, semi-romantic evening out: a little dinner, a deep conversation, planning on going to some sickeningly romantic movie. It promised to be a truly unforgettable evening—and that's exactly what it became.

We went to eat at one of those Shogun Japanese steak houses where an authentic samurai-style chef comes out armed with a sword, a spatula, and a tall hat. He slices, dices, and prepares your meal right in front of you. It's all very exciting.

As we sat next to a giant aquarium full of sickly looking fish, our chef juggled our steak, seafood, and vegetables. (I guess it's all right to play with someone else's food, just not your own.) He threw sharp knives and salt shakers around just inches away from our faces. This meal was death-defying stuff. Finally he finished the show, and we got to eat.

I was starving by then so I quickly inhaled my meat, veggies, and fried rice. We were having a great time. I was enjoying spending some time with my beautiful wife. But all of that was about to be shattered by a rumbling in my stomach. I tried to ignore it. I sat there and drank a little hot tea. But the rumbling got louder and more violent. It became painfully obvious something in my tummy was desperately trying to fight its way out. I knew if I didn't find a bathroom right away, things were going to get ugly.

I tried to quietly excuse myself. I walked briskly to the men's restroom, reached down to open the door, and found it locked. The restroom was occupied; this was terrible. I could feel my colon about to make a serious download, and I knew time was running out. I knocked on the bathroom door and heard a raspy voice inside say, "Hold on, partner—I'll be out in a few minutes."

A few minutes? I didn't have a few minutes.

I looked over and noticed that the women's bathroom door was cracked open. I assumed this meant no one was in there. So I waddled over and swung open the door, only to discover that someone *was* in there. She screamed and let the entire restaurant know I was a filthy pervert.

I did the "trying to take my mind off this" dance, but it didn't work. It was bad. I tightened every muscle in my body, hoping this would somehow hold things off. I heard the guy in the men's restroom flush. Then he started washing his hands and whistling. He was whistling! I couldn't believe it.

Finally he began to open the door. It seemed like everything was in slow motion. He was an elderly man wearing a cowboy hat. He looked at me and said, "I don't know what your cotton-pickin' hurry was."

At that precise moment, when I was just inches away from the porcelain promised land, my body reached the point of no control. I lost control, and my muscles, which up to this point had fought a brave battle to contain the coming flood, gave up. Right there in a Japanese restaurant in Arlington, Texas, I soiled my shorts—and I mean *violently*.

I made a sad, futile attempt to clean myself up. Then I tried to walk out like nothing had happened. Diana said, "Hey, Babe, do you want dessert?"

I looked at her with a pained expression and said in a hushed tone, "I pooped my pants."

She said, "What did you say?"

I replied, "*I...pooped...my...pants!*"

She looked at me with a compassionate yet confused look and said, "Eeww!" We walked out of there, trying not to draw any attention to me or my defiled pants. The hostess, who was wearing a brightly colored kimono, said, "Thank you. Have a nice evening."

I looked at her and said, "*Arigato.*"

⟫ Something to Stand On

Epilogue (or why in the world I would tell this story)

I know what you're thinking: *Man, that's gross. I've lost all respect for you, Luke. Why would you include this story?*

Here's why. A few weeks after this incident, I was speaking at a youth rally. I shared this story, and it seriously disturbed some people. But one disheveled-looking junior high boy came up to me and said, "You know, I pooped my pants a while back, and I thought I was the biggest loser in the world. And then I heard your story, and I realized everybody does that once in a while, and I realized I'm okay."

That, my friend, is why I share this story—and my other stories. Because maybe, just maybe it will make someone realize she's okay. You can feel amazing liberation in knowing you're not the only one who has messed up or failed or disappointed someone.

Four of the most powerful words in the English language are *You are not alone*. When we become vulnerable and completely honest, we open the door for others to identify with our mistakes or struggles. That opens the door for healing to happen. This is how we turn failure into fruit.

But too often we try to maintain the perfect facade, and we're afraid to let people know we stumble and sin and soil ourselves. I'm not willing or wired to play that game anymore. If by exposing my shortcomings, someone else can find hope, humor, and healing, then I'll do it. (I think that's fairly obvious now.)

Something amazing happens when I admit to myself and those around me that despite my hard work and best intentions, I'm not cool and I won't ever be cool—and it's okay. Because God, who knows me more than anyone, accepts me, even when I soil myself, and he loves me. And not only does God love me, but he also likes me. And he feels the same way about you. When we're honest and open about our weaknesses, God's strength is truly allowed to show through us.

Noah was a kid who was allergic to many things
From milk to grass and eggs and fried onion rings.

These things made him sneeze and break out in red spots.
We've never counted them; let's just say there are lots!

And when it gets really bad, Noah gets itchy lumps
Which, in the right lighting, look just like little chicken rumps.

His folks don't know if they should take him to get shots
Or grab an ink pen and play connect the dots.

There are lots of things that don't give Noah bumps.
So he dwells on those items instead of getting in the dumps.

Noah likes soy burgers, water parks, and fun.
Laughter, oatmeal, cartoons, and midday sun.

Sometimes life gives a bump, lump, or stump,
Things that, if you let them, can make you a grump.

The worst allergies can't be seen, not even if you're cross-eyed.
They're sticky and invisible and make you bumpy on the inside.

Things like fear, doubt, wrong choices, and pride,
Phoniness, prejudice, and selfishness leave you fried.

Take it from me: As much as you're able,
Always try to keep these things off of your table.

Focus on what you can do. Find your niche.
And by all means avoid things that will make you itch!

chapter nineteen
Cow Manure and Grace

We were taking a break from the urban jungle and visiting some of our favorite people, Dennis and Charlotte Berry. They live in one of the coolest places on the planet: Crabtree, Arkansas, which, for your information, is just a few miles north of Toadsuck, Arkansas... seriously. I didn't make that up. They live out in the country on top of an incredibly beautiful mountain.

It was a great day. The sun was shining. The birds were singing. We were surrounded by actual trees and other assorted live examples of nature—it was beautiful.

We went out in their pasture. They had some baby calves, and we were getting to feed them with what looked like huge baby bottles. It was very cool.

Delanie was about three years old at the time. The whole nature thing was pretty new to her because at the time she was a serious city kid. She'd been raised around concrete not cows, so she wasn't real nature savvy. She was just toddling around the pasture when she saw something she didn't recognize. It was large and round and brown. It looked a little like play dough, so she bent over to investigate. She looked at the brown dough, and it looked harmless enough.

So she reached out and grabbed a chunky handful of the mystery substance. She lifted it up to her face to get a closer look. Then after getting a really good smell, she realized she was holding a handful of fresh cow manure. She looked up with a confused look on her face and asked, "Poopy?"

Delanie was naturally upset because she was (and is) a very sanitary child who normally didn't enjoy playing with manure. She started to cry and shout, "POOPY!" She instinctively reached up to wipe her tears—with her chubby, little now-brown hand—and she got manure all over her face and in her hair.

This upset her even more, and she started jumping up and down and shouting, "POOPY! POOPY! POOPY!" She was flinging the stuff all around. It was amazing, because it really seemed as if the cow manure was multiplying. Somehow she had it all over her head, clothes, and little body. She looked like an angry little manure monster.

At that precise moment my daughter noticed me standing there, just watching her. She scurried over to me, lifted

Cow Manure and Grace

up her arms, and said, "Daddy, hold me." I looked down at my distraught baby girl, and I said, "*No.*" I know it was harsh, but she was covered head to toe. I, on the other hand, was not and wanted to stay that way.

Something had changed between my daughter and me. It wasn't my love for her. I didn't care for her any less. I still loved her completely. I would still do anything for her. Even with manure all over her, I would still die for her. Our relationship hadn't changed. She was still my daughter, and I was still her daddy. I didn't disown her or kick her out of the family.

But something had changed. Our level of intimacy had been seriously affected. We couldn't get close at that moment because something in her life was prohibiting it. Cow manure was keeping us from being close.

I found an easy solution to all of this. I took a long green garden hose and sprayed her off. I cleaned her up. Then I picked her up and gave her a big hug.

⫸ Something to Stand On

I've been a follower of Christ for quite a while. A lot of times I know I've disappointed or disobeyed God. I've played with "spiritual poopy," and I've wondered if I've wandered outside the limits of God's mercy.

While I was standing there in a cow pasture with my three-year-old, I learned a huge lesson about grace. When I made a decision to follow Jesus, I was adopted into God's family. I'm God's child. It really is just that simple. Still, I sin; I blow it; I end up covered in spiritual manure.

As an earthly father I'm supposed to be a pale reflection of the heavenly Father. That afternoon in Arkansas I learned something about dads. I realized even when I make stupid choices and think surely I've blown it beyond repair, my Father loves me. *Nothing* can separate me from God's love. The Bible puts it like this: "For I am convinced that neither death nor life, neither angels nor demons, neither the present nor the future, nor any powers, neither height nor depth, nor anything else in all creation, will be able to separate us from the love of God that is in Christ Jesus our Lord" (Romans 8:38-39). God's love for me is stronger and more powerful than any stupid thing I have done or will do. It's like super-powered Velcro love. It sticks to me no matter what. I can't make God *not* love me. He also doesn't disown me when I disappoint him. He's still my Father; I'm still his child.

When I mess up, what changes is our level of intimacy. We aren't touching like we once were. But that's easily remedied. I just need to get cleaned up. Just as I did with Delanie, God cleans me up. I can't clean myself up. All I can do is go to him, admit I'm filthy, and ask him for help.

Sin is a seriously huge deal that affects our relationship with God and other people. But the Bible tells us how to deal with it: "If we confess our sins, he is faithful and just and will forgive us our sins and purify us from all unrighteousness" (1 John 1:9). This verse is our escape hatch. It lets us know we can conquer the harsh reality of sin.

I don't know what you've done. Maybe you were close to God at one time, but you've made some stupid choices—welcome to the club. Maybe you've never made the choice to follow Christ, or maybe everything is fine in your spiritual life. Wherever you are, let me tell you this: The One who created you and knows you better than anyone else wants to have a continuous, intimate relationship with you. Nothing you've done is bigger or stronger than God's love for you. Quit playing in the poopy in your life, let God wash you clean, and enjoy his love for you.

chapter twenty
That's It...I'm Putting Myself up for Adoption!

Most of us have probably clung to the hope of adoption at one time or another to justify our warped family situation. "Okay, I can't relate to my mom; I'm nothing like my dad; and I don't really look like my brother—I must be adopted. That would explain everything." Then we take it a little further, and we imagine our birth parents were good-looking, mega-talented, interesting celebrities or world leaders who only gave us up because they somehow loved us too much. We use the idea of adoption to explain away our differences.

As someone who spent a good chunk of his life looking for belonging, the concept of adoption totally amazes me. Think about it—it's the idea of finding a family and a future. Isn't that what we all crave? I've seen adoption up close and personal a couple of times in my life.

The first time was when I was in fourth grade. My parents adopted my sister Hope. She came from Korea. At the time I had no idea where Korea was. I knew it was a long way off—probably near Cleveland. Hope was 14 months old when she came to America and became a part of our family. She was brought over from Seoul by a chaperone from the adoption agency.

Her chaperone was a little old Korean lady. The chaperone was about four feet tall and seemed very angry. She was holding my sister away from her body like she was radioactive. It turned out they'd run out of clean diapers somewhere over the Pacific, so my sister had gone hours without getting her diaper changed and smelled like about 22 pounds of toxic waste. Also, she had chicken pox. So for some medicinal reason, they had shaved the back of her head, and she had what looked a little like a sideways Mohawk.

Hope had lived in a little orphanage in Korea for 14 months, so she wasn't used to a bunch of overexcited white people—she really didn't want to have anything to do with any of us. The first time I met my sister, she was a stinky, little, polka-dotted, half-bald, cranky toddler, but none of that mattered. She was my sister. She was instantly a member of our family.

My sister's adoption was a very deliberate thing. My parents had planned it for about two years. They'd filled out mountains of paperwork. They'd seen baby pictures. She was chosen. She found her place, for better or worse, in our family, and we watched her grow into an incredible young lady.

It's no major revelation to most people who meet our family that Hope is adopted—most people can figure it out pretty quick. She's a tall, beautiful, gifted, sophisticated Asian. I'm a short, odd-looking, goofy white guy.

My second up-close experience with adoption was a few years ago. Doug and Kimberly Uyechi are some of our best friends. They're two very gifted and compassionate people. They had been married for years and wanted a child. If there ever was a couple who would make great parents, it was Doug and Kimberly. They had so much love to give, but it wasn't happening. They went through years of heartache and disappointment as they watched others have babies. They tried and did everything they could, but it just didn't happen.

After much prayer and thought, they decided to adopt. Through some contacts at church, they met an unwed teen mother who wasn't going to be able to take care of her baby. They went through all the preparation and planning, and God gave them a beautiful baby boy. They were there the day he was born. Incidentally, my family was at the hospital that day, too. It was big stuff, and we weren't going to miss it.

We all welcomed their son, Keoni, to this planet. Keoni didn't realize it that day—someday he probably will—but he hit the jackpot. Keoni got two of the greatest parents ever. He is loved, protected, and provided for. It's the only life he's ever known. He was rescued and given a family and a future.

Something to Stand On

Isn't that what we're all looking for? We want a place to belong and a reason to live. That's what our Creator offers us. I think it's incredibly significant that when describing our relationship with God, the Bible compares it to adoption. Look at this super-chunky Bible passage: "Even before he made the world, God loved us and chose us in Christ to be holy and without fault in his eyes. God decided in advance to adopt us into his own family by bringing us to himself through Jesus Christ. This is what he wanted to do, and it gave him great pleasure" (Ephesians 1:4-5, NLT).

We can make becoming a Christ-follower seem like joining a club or signing a contract. We can turn it into some hyped-up sales pitch. But God, who started this whole faith thing, uses the concept of adoption to paint the picture of us becoming a part of his family—not his club.

That was God's "unchanging plan" to bring us into his tribe.

We've been adopted into the family of God. I think God used the picture of adoption on purpose to show us the great thought and effort he put into getting us into his family. Adoption is a very carefully planned, thought-out thing.

Nobody is accidental. God has a purpose for everyone who is born. No one is a mistake or a mishap. But there are unplanned births. I was one. (Remember chapter one?) But there's never been an unplanned adoption. Nobody ever wakes up and says, "Whoa! We adopted a kid. How did that happen?"

Food for Freaks

One of my favorite vegetables—or it might be a fruit; I'm really not sure—is the avocado. I love avocados. They're an edible object lesson about God's grace and creativity.

Avocados aren't pretty. In fact they're quite possibly the ugliest food on the planet. They come in various shades of brownish green and greenish brown. They're slimy and oddly shaped. Yet out of this incredibly unsightly vegetable (or fruit) comes something delicious and refreshing.

I've felt like an avocado many times in my life. I've had countless ugly moments when I feel slimy and oddly shaped—especially when I'm wearing a swimsuit, but that's beside the point. Yet out of my life God brings forth something good and refreshing. Avocados give us hope. True beauty has more to do with our flavor than our looks: "But we have this treasure in jars of clay to show that this all-surpassing power is from God and not from us" (2 Corinthians 4:7).

My parents put great time and effort into adopting my sister. They invested financial and emotional resources. There was no planning in my becoming a part of the family, just some unleashed teenage hormones in the backseat of an old car.

God has made a way for you to be a part of his family. He did it on purpose. It was no accident or afterthought. He put great thought into it. He paid a huge price to adopt you. God has a place for you. God adopts us. He rescues us and gives us a family and a future.

We find something that was lost and stolen from us. We find a place to belong; we find purpose. We hit the jackpot! Even if we're stinky, polka-dotted, half-bald, little, cranky people, we instantly become full-fledged members of the family. God tells us,

"So you have not received a spirit that makes you fearful slaves. Instead, you received God's Spirit when he adopted you as his own children. Now we call him, 'Abba, Father.'" (Romans 8:15, NLT).

chapter twenty-one

Twister

It was April 24, 1993, and Diana and I were youth pastors at a church in Tulsa. We lived in a little bitty house on the church grounds. The house was roughly the exact same size and shape as an average shoe box.

It was a Saturday evening around 6:30 p.m., and I'd just gotten home from work. I worked at a bookstore. Diana, who we had just found out was pregnant, was away at a women's conference in Texas. I was all alone, and I had some big plans. I was going to eat some hearty, manly grub—a delicious and nutritious Hungry Man salisbury steak TV dinner—and I was going to watch professional wrestling and make manly noises. It doesn't get much better than that.

When I got home I noticed the sky looked really weird. It was almost a surreal shade of gray. I turned on the TV, and the high-strung local weatherman was nervously talking about storm fronts and funnel clouds and possible tornadic activity. If you live in Oklahoma for any amount of time, you get used to the threat of tornadoes. I put my Hungry Man meal in the microwave and set the timer. I was about to assume my rightful position in the recliner with a remote control in my hand when the silence was broken by some loud sirens going off right outside.

Howard and Catherine Mabry, the pastors, lived right next door to us in an identical shoe box house. Howard and Catherine were great people who had been pastors for about 50 years. They loved people, and they loved Jesus.

When the sirens starting blaring, I called them, and Catherine answered. I said, "What is that?"

She replied, "Well, it's a tornado."

I said, "Oh, what do I do?"

She answered, "Get somewhere!" Then she hung up— evidently so she could get somewhere herself.

The wind was really picking up outside, so I decided I really ought to get somewhere, although I didn't know where to get. I remembered hearing somewhere that the bathroom was the safest room in the house, which is reassuring because I spend a lot of time there. I ran in and knelt down by the tub.

The weather was actually getting pretty scary at this point. It was getting noisier, and the wind was getting stronger. I started praying hard and fast. I was pleading with God for protection. I just wanted to see my wife. I wanted to be around to meet my unborn child. I could hear and feel things banging up against the side of our little house. It sounded like a freight train was going right through our living room. I was facedown on our bathroom floor, shaking and shivering and crying out for divine assistance.

It's during times like this, when all pretense and pride is stripped away, that you realize what's really important in life. It's just you and God and a storm, and you realize what matters most—and it wasn't what I was wearing or driving. It didn't matter where we lived or that we only had $2.37 in our checking account. It was pretty simple: What mattered was my family and my faith, and that was it.

Then just as quickly as the storm started, it ended, and there was a tangible stillness all around me. I lay there on the bathroom floor for a while. When I was able to finally get up, I realized our little house was intact.

I walked outside, and it looked almost like a war zone. Howard and Catherine were fine, although the tornado had demolished Catherine's little storage building. She had kept 40 years worth of sewing and craft supplies in it, so there were strands of fabric everywhere. Broken glass and wood were everywhere. Large chunks of other people's houses were in our front yards. The storm had knocked out the windows in our cars and knocked the steeple off the church. The wooden playground and jungle gym were totally gone. We walked around, trying to take it all in.

The tornado hit a large truck stop right across the highway from us. It killed 16 people there. People who were just trying to get home. These people were parents, grandparents, children, brothers, and sisters. They had plans and dreams, but these plans came to an ugly end on a spring

Twister

day in Tulsa. The truck stop was totally wiped out. Twisted steel and destruction were everywhere. Yet right where the truck stop kitchen had been minutes before, there was a Styrofoam container of eggs just sitting there, and not one of the eggs was even cracked.

I sat in my living room in the dark watching the fire trucks, ambulances, and helicopters come and go. I thought about how life can change in an instant. We make our plans, but in the blink of an eye, everything can be turned upside down.

≫ Something to Stand On

The wisest investments are made in the things that matter most. When we're shaken to our foundations, suddenly fashion, popularity, fame, and mutual funds don't really matter at all. We're left holding onto our faith, our family, and our friends—and that's about it.

If that's what matters when the storm hits, why can't we live for those things when everything is fine? Why do we allow ourselves to be distracted by things that don't matter?

I've been through many storms since that day in 1993. They all take me back to a desperate little man lying on a bathroom floor and the clarity about what matters that I gained there.

There is a thing that lives under my bed.
A super-scary monster that fills me with dread.

I've never seen it, but I've heard it once or twice.
I dream about it every night, and believe me, it's not nice!

It looks like a giant, vicious mothball with teeth.
It waits below my bunk to attack from underneath.

For years I have lived with this ever-present fright.
That's why I can't sleep without my trusty night-light.

I lie at least six inches from the edge of my bed,
Out of reach so the thing can't grab me by the head.

I finally decided I couldn't take anymore!
I had to know what lived on my bedroom floor.

So I got up my nerve and looked under the bed.
What I saw there surprised me and made my face turn red.

There was a red shoe, some broken toys, and dust bunnies,
A half-eaten sandwich and two pages of funnies.

Even though I didn't see the thing, I was sure it was there
Probably hiding behind old Spider-Man underwear.

Taking a deep breath, I had to know the truth at last.
So I looked closer, for I had a mothball monster to unmask!

I knew what I must do. I mustered courage and grit.
I faced my biggest fear, and there was nothing to it!

I looked all around, found no monsters, just stuff.
I couldn't believe it! I had called the thing's bluff!

Last night I slept close to the edge the first time.
Turns out the mothball monster was all in my mind.

RIPOFF'S BELIEVE IT OR DON'T!!!
FOR THE LAST 27 YEARS NORMA PORKMEYER, OF OXBELCH, IOWA, HAS MADE ALL OF HER OWN CLOTHING ENTIRELY OUT OF USED DENTAL FLOSS! BELIEVE IT OR DON'T!
THAT MAKES HER THE LEADER OF THE PLAQUE.

chapter twenty-two

Lessons from Dad

On November 28, 2000, my dad, Delano Lang, went to heaven. He had a massive heart attack and was unconscious for eight days. We surrounded his bedside, and we prayed and hoped and remembered and cried and laughed.

When the end (actually, it was the beginning) came, we gained a clear, undeniable glimpse into the unseen world. We were all standing there, and it was obvious when Dad left the building. We could sense the very second he passed. No doctor had to tell us. One second he was there; the next he was gone. He vacated his earthly dwelling to move to a much better neighborhood.

We let him go. During the preceding eight days, we had learned what real trust in an unseen God is. We learned that if we really believed what we had professed for years, we would let Dad go. Besides, it wasn't good-bye—it was just see you later.

And as we said "See you later," we felt a strong, tangible sense of the holy in that hospital room. We joined hands and sang "God Is Good All the Time" because he is. I've never been more sure of the fact that this life isn't all there is than at that moment.

>>> Something to Stand On

My dad was no mere mortal. He was John Wayne and Superman all rolled into one big, hairy package. When I was a kid, I was sure Dad was invincible. Even when I was older, I felt completely safe whenever he was around. I found out later he wasn't invincible. But in my mind he'll always be the strongest, smartest, toughest man I'll ever meet.

I remember so much about Dad. I remember his laugh, the way he wore his hat, and the way he smelled. I remember his bushy eyebrows that by looking angry could paralyze me with fear. I remember his hands covered in calluses from hard work. I remember the lessons he tried to teach me that never stuck, like how to work on cars or how to be a handyman. I never really caught either of those.

But I also remember all of the things he taught me that did stick. He taught me how to be a man. Without ever claiming to be a leader, he taught me more about leadership than anyone else. He taught me what integrity, respect, work ethic, and honor are all about.

Dad was a man of few words. As I was growing up, it seemed like he communicated mainly through grunts.

A happy grunt meant he was pleased; an unhappy grunt meant someone was in big trouble. Most of what he taught me was through his example and not his words. He modeled life for me, and some of the time, I caught it.

As I reflected on the mostly nonverbal instruction my father gave me, I realized some other life lessons he taught me:

- Get your priorities right: God first, your family second, your friends third, and yourself fourth.

- Authentic faith isn't just something you talk about. It's something that affects every area of your life.

- Work hard, play hard, and take a nap every once in a while.

- Be the first to leave the party—it leaves people wanting more.

- True wealth has nothing to do with material possessions or bank accounts. It has to do with what you deposit in the lives of those around you.

- Real friends stick with you through the tough times. Remember to return the favor.

- There's always plenty of blame to pass around; but don't do it—take responsibility.

- Look people in the eye and tell the truth.

- The right thing and the hardest thing are usually the same thing.

- Live every moment to the fullest. There's something much worse than dying—not living.

- Don't play favorites—treat everyone the same.
- A life lived for others is never in vain.
- There is never a bad time for breakfast.
- It's better to fail than to quit.
- If you tell people the truth the first time, you won't have to apologize or backtrack later.
- Appreciate and enjoy simple things.
- Live with repentance instead of regret so you can die with faith instead of fear.
- Live in such a way that you leave a mark.
- Appreciate nature.
- Everything's better with gravy on it.
- Read just for fun.
- Honesty is more important than perfection.
- Plain white T's, baseball caps, and pearl-snap shirts never go out of style. (Okay, maybe they do, but who cares?)
- Laugh often.
- Live for something bigger than yourself.

Thanks, Dad. I miss you, but I'll see you soon.

chapter twenty-three

The Prayer of Saint Pete

I love the Bible. It's the story of flawed people connecting with a flawless God. No matter who you are, the Bible has someone you can relate to.

A lot of people assume, for some fairly obvious reasons, that my favorite Bible character is Zacchaeus (the famous biblical short guy). Although Zac is definitely in my top five, my fave and the dude I can absolutely relate to is a guy named Simon Peter. Peter is the patron saint of failures, freaks, and flunkies everywhere.

Peter was a big, burly fisherman. Fishermen weren't known for their social skills. They smelled like...well...fish. They didn't get invited to a lot of parties. Fishermen were rough, tough men. In all probability they were a little rude and crude. Their language wasn't flowery or kid friendly. Their humor was raw. They probably laughed at the same stuff as most 13-year-old boys ("Hey, Peter, pull my finger!"), yet these were the people Jesus chose to hang out with. Hmmm...kind of makes you think.

Peter was impulsive and probably a little loud and obnoxious. He had a good heart and good intentions, but he was always saying or doing the wrong thing. He did a lot of stupid stuff because he didn't think before he acted. He was constantly putting his foot in his mouth and embarrassing himself and everyone around him. Can you see why I can totally relate to this dude?

The story of Peter gives me hope. He failed, he fell, he flopped—yet he was a friend of God. He was a walking, talking social blunder, yet God did amazing things to him and through him.

⫸ Something to Stand On

There is one particular story in which Pete shows us what I feel is one of the most power-packed prayers of all time. How's that for hype?

You can find the whole story in Matthew 14:22-31. But let me break it down for you a bit. After a physically grueling day of ministry, Jesus needed a little alone time, so he sent the disciples in a boat ahead to the other side of the lake. He had his own travel plans; he planned to walk *across the lake*.

At about three in the morning, a storm broke out, and the disciples were scared. They looked up, and through the rain, mist, and choppy waves, they saw someone or something walking toward them. So they were freaked. Was it a ghost? Was it some kind of walking sea zombie? Turned out it was Jesus. He was just out taking a stroll—across the lake!

All of the previously freaked disciples got quiet all of a sudden. They really weren't sure what to do with this spectacle, except for Peter, who spoke up: "That's cool. I want to walk on water, too."

Jesus extended his hand and said, "Come on; let's take a little walk."

By the way, I think it's sad at this point that Peter was the only one who got out of the boat. Everyone else just decided to watch. But Peter hopped up and out onto the waves and started walking. But then, out of the corner of his eye, he saw the gnarly waves and felt the mist on his face. He probably realized how crazy he looked, and suddenly, things felt out of his control—and he started to sink.

Glub...glub...glub...(those are written sound effects). So he shouted a desperate three-word prayer: "Lord, save me!" And Jesus, who is truly the most amazing lifeguard ever (sorry, David Hasselhoff), reached down and saved him.

I love the prayer of Saint Pete. "Lord, save me!" It's just three words. It's one of the shortest yet most effective prayers of all time.

"Lord, save me!" It's not pretty. It's not complicated.

"Lord, save me!" It's not long or wordy. There's no time for that.

"Lord, save me!" There's no bargaining with God because you realize you have nothing to offer.

"Lord, save me!" It's honest and desperate. Millions of people have prayed the same prayer.

"Lord, save me!"

How about you?

Are things out of your control? Do you feel like you're sinking?

"Lord, save me!"

Glub...glub...glub...

"Lord, save me!"

The World's Shortest Self-Help Book

"Forget about self-confidence; it's useless. Cultivate God-confidence." (1 Corinthians 10:12, MSG)

That's it.

The Art of Conformity

> *I spent years being told to shut up and conform. Don't be different; don't make waves. Dress like everybody else. Follow the rules. Think like everybody else. Act like everybody else.*

But if you follow all of that advice, life becomes one big dress code. I've never been a big fan of dress codes. They're not just high school deals, either. Go to most offices or churches, and you'll find people all dressed alike—not because they want to, but because it's the norm.

I hate dress clothes. They never fit me right, especially dress pants. They make me itchy and uncomfortable. Nothing ever looks right, either. Everything I wear looks baggy because I have a baggy body.

One day I realized I didn't want to conform. I saw conformity as a vicious circle that never lets up. It's like a really crowded, out-of-control playground merry-go-round. You frantically try to look and act like everyone else and forget who you really are. And fashion constantly changes, so you're constantly forced to redefine yourself. I hear people say they dress a certain way because they want to express themselves—yet they express themselves by looking, acting, and thinking like everyone else. That's a little messed up.

I didn't want to be like everybody else—that's boring. I wanted to be me. Even now I still dress like I did when I was 12. I wear wrinkled T-shirts (preferably with a picture of a superhero or one of my favorite sports teams), baggy shorts, and Chuck Taylor high-tops.

The problem is that somewhere along the line, we start to believe being different is somehow bad. We think the key to survival and acceptance is conformity. We should all work hard to look, act, and think the same. But the truth is, different is good. Different is proof we have a Creator who has a wild imagination and a great sense of humor.

Be yourself. Don't let anyone press you into some stupid mold. Maybe you look or dress different than anyone else. Maybe you act or think a little different than other people; maybe you don't. As long as you're being yourself, it really is all good.

Here's an actual fact that hopefully sets you at ease: God doesn't want you to be anything or anybody you aren't. Just be yourself for God. Be yourself for himself. When we decide to live for him, God doesn't change our passions or personality. He changes our purpose and our priorities. He knows you. So be who God made you to be.

The Art of Conformity

We were all designed to be different. A soup or stew with only one ingredient would be pretty bland. The variety of ingredients is what makes things tasty. Be yourself, for therein lies the magic and a miracle. As you encounter and eventually embrace who you were born to be, miraculous things take place. You're set free from the chains of conformity.

Conformity is the natural enemy of creativity. I refuse to conform because I'm a piece of art. I'm a priceless, one-of-a-kind masterpiece—and so are you.

You might not feel like a masterpiece, but you are. You might feel your life is anything but art right now. That's only because you're too close to yourself.

≫≫ Something to Stand On

I live just a few miles away from an amazing art gallery. It's an incredible place that inspires the snot out of me (not literally...that would be gross). Now imagine you're at the art museum, and you walk right up to a framed painting. You get so close to the painting your nose is touching it. It's a beautiful painting of a nature scene complete with thick green grass, a babbling waterfall, and big oak trees with a chubby brown squirrel sitting on a branch. But you can't appreciate the painting because you're too close. All you can see is a green blur, a skinny blue mark, and a brown spot. It makes no sense because your perspective is all messed up. But if you step back a few feet, everything starts to take shape, and you can see the waterfall and the tree and even the cute little squirrel.

Life can be the same. You don't realize that you're too close to see the whole picture clearly. As you get older and get a little more perspective, things will start shaping up.

You also need to remember that not only are you a masterpiece, but everybody you know is also a masterpiece. Everyone on this planet is art, whether they act like it or not. So you need to treat them like art. We need to give others the space and the grace to be themselves. That means we don't put down or disrespect the art in others.

Imagine once again you're back at the art gallery, and there's a big opening. An amazing artist is there showing off some of his favorite work. You walk in and walk up to a piece, clear your throat, and spit on his painting (shocking, isn't it?). How do you think the artist would feel? Hurt? Angry? Disrespected? If you disrespect the creation, you're disrespecting the creator.

When we disrespect people, the walking, talking art around us, we're disrespecting the Creator, the artist who crafted them. I think God takes that personally. Allow others to be themselves.

Conformity really is a crime against the Creator. To be anything other than yourself is to deny the divine. God has unleashed amazing creative diversity and wild beauty in you. For us to try to contain the creativity just isn't right.

chapter twenty-six

Freak of Nature

I think I have proven beyond a shadow of a doubt that I am truly a freak of nature, and that's okay. I enjoy my freaky life.

I don't know what the freak factor is in your life. You might be fairly normal—and that's completely okay, too—but no matter who you are, let me download a fact into your life. You might not be a genetic or social freak of nature, but if you're a Christ follower, then, whether you realize it or not, you're a spiritual freak of nature.

Galatians 5:16-18 says, "So I say, let the Holy Spirit guide your lives. Then you won't be doing what your sinful nature craves. The sinful nature wants to do evil, which is just the opposite of what the Spirit wants. And the Spirit gives us desires that are the opposite of what the sinful nature desires. These two forces are constantly fighting each other, so you are not free to carry out your good intentions. But when you are directed by the Holy Spirit, you are not under obligation to the law of Moses" (NLT).

You become a spiritual freak of nature when you decide to rebel against your old nature and allow the Holy Spirit to control your life. Your old nature tells you to serve and satisfy yourself and live selfishly. The Holy Spirit always urges us to serve and satisfy God and live unselfishly.

We have to decide daily that we're going to allow the Holy Spirit to direct us and help us make the right choices. When we do that, we're taking our lives to an exciting new level. We aren't living in the natural anymore. We're living in the supernatural. We've supersized our lives.

You can't really serve God by doing what comes naturally. Instead of living for him, you naturally want to live for yourself. You naturally want to satisfy and feed your urges and desires. It's easy just to give in and live naturally and not think for yourself or practice spiritual discipline. It's easy to live naturally and not worry about other people. It's easy to live naturally and not make any efforts for spiritual or social change. It's entirely too easy to live naturally and do whatever feels right or pleasurable to you.

The hard, cold truth is, living naturally will jack you up. Every problem that we have in the world today can be traced to someone who did what came naturally. Not only will living naturally bring us trouble and heartache, but doing what comes naturally will also eventually kill us. The Bible says, "The wages of sin is death" (Romans 6:23).

When you choose to be a freak of nature, you decide to supersize your life, dreams, and future. Freak out—rebel against yourself. Reject your old nature and live in the realm of the supernatural.

Freaks of nature, unite!

Viva la freak!

chapter twenty-seven

I AM Standing Up!

Let me describe what has become a common scenario in my life. It usually happens in a very public setting. I will be minding my business, and somebody will introduce or point me out and say, "Stand up, Luke. Oh, you are standing up." Whoever says it thinks he's being really clever and witty. On the outside I usually laugh along. "Ha, ha, oh boy, that's funny." But on the inside I'm thinking, Sheesh! I've only heard that about 57 million times.

In fact I've heard it so many times, it's almost become a mantra to me: I AM standing up! It's something I now tell myself often. Life isn't easy. Sometimes it's really hard, but I am standing up. I've been verbally assaulted and attacked, but I am standing up. I have been at the edge of ruin, but I didn't give up...I am standing up. I've been lied to and lied about, but I am standing up. I have been hurt, humiliated, and humbled, but I am standing up. I've been knocked down, but I'm not staying down...I am standing up. The enemy has tried to steal, kill, and destroy my life and dreams, but he hasn't succeeded. I AM standing up!

I know deep in my heart that without Christ I can do nothing. I've proven that over and over. I desperately, continually need him. Without him I can't stand; I fall on my face. I am standing up only because he gives me the strength to stand *and* he stands with me always. I am standing up on his Word and what it says about me. His Word tells me that through Christ I can do all things. Through Christ I have hope and a future.

Here's a profound thought: In the Old Testament when God wanted to reveal part of himself to the Israelites, he told them his name was "I AM." Exodus 3:14-15 says, "God said to Moses, 'I AM WHO I AM. This is what you are to say to the Israelites: "I AM has sent me to you"'... This is my name forever, the name you shall call me from generation to generation."

So, I AM standing up. "The Great I AM," the ever-present, eternal Creator and King of all things is standing up for me and in me and through me.

The Bible is an amazingly honest and relevant book. It's full of messed-up people, whacked-out situations, and dysfunctional families. The good news is that through living in relationship with our Creator we can stand up in the middle of the mess.

The message of the Bible is that not only can Jesus rescue us from hell when we die, but knowing him also makes our lives better now. We can know him, and that gives us hope and significance. And it should affect the way we live and the way we treat the people around us. God helps our lives make sense. He helps us matter. Because of that, I am standing up.

I'm sure your life isn't always fair or easy. I know you probably have more than your share of pain, problems, and obstacles. That's not a prophetic thing or amazing insight on my part—it's just life on a fallen planet. Maybe you, too, are a freak. I know sometimes life just really does stink. But as a fellow freak, I encourage you to stand up. Don't sit down, don't give up—stand up. And keep standing up. You'll have situations that can knock you down. Don't let that happen—stand!

"So then, brothers and sisters, stand firm and hold fast to the teachings we passed on to you, whether by word of mouth or by letter. May our Lord Jesus Christ himself and God our Father, who loved us and by his grace gave us eternal encouragement and good hope, encourage your hearts and strengthen you in every good deed and word" (2 Thessalonians 2:15-17).

Say it with me:

I am standing up!

I AM standing up!

I am STANDING up!

I am standing UP!

> I AM STANDING UP!
>
> Now—
>
> STAND!

The Wisdom On... series is designed to help you apply biblical wisdom to your everyday life. You'll find case studies, personal inventories, interactive activities, and helpful insights from the book of Proverbs, which will show you what wise living looks like.

Wisdom On...Friends, Dating, and Relationships
ISBN 978-0-310-27927-3

Wisdom On...Getting Along with Parents
ISBN 978-0-310-27929-7

Wisdom On...Growing in Christ
ISBN 978-0-310-27932-7

Wisdom On...Making Good Decisions
ISBN 978-0-310-27926-6

Wisdom On...Music, Movies, & Television
ISBN 978-0-310-27931-0

Wisdom On...Time & Money
ISBN 978-0-310-27928-0

Mark Matlock
RETAIL $9.99

Visit www.planetwisdom.com or your local bookstore.

Our planet is no longer the paradise God created. In *It's Easy Being Green*, you'll learn how to honor God in the choices you make, and you'll begin to understand the impact those choices have on the environment. Sixteen-year-old Emma Sleeth will help you see how you can make a difference at school, around the house, and all over the world.

It's Easy Being Green
One Student's Guide to Serving God and Saving the Planet
Emma Sleeth
RETAIL $12.99
ISBN 978-0-310-27925-9

Visit www.planetwisdom.com or your local bookstore.

With all the demands in your life, it's easy to sometimes feel small, worried, or weak, or even struggle with feeling unforgivable, tempted, or worthless. In this book, you'll discover that you're not alone (and you're perfectly normal!), and you'll also find your true identity in the God who created you.

You Are Not Alone
Seeing Your Struggles Through the Eyes of God
Shirley Perich
RETAIL $9.99
ISBN 978-0-310-28532-8

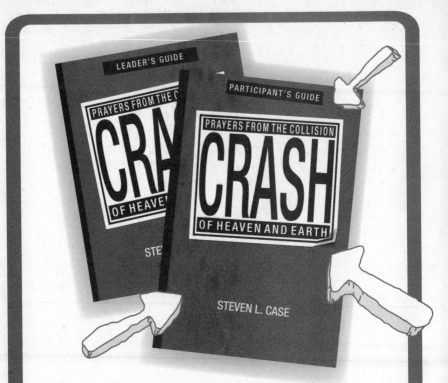

This book is a guide to help you live your life inside the crash—
the collision that takes place every time we pray for God's will to
be done on earth. Unlike any other book on prayer, this is more
like an experience of the power of prayer. See what the world
looks like at the point of impact.

Crash Participant's Guide
Prayers from the Collision of Heaven and Earth
Steven L. Case
RETAIL $9.99
ISBN 978-0-310-28775-9

Crash
Prayers from the Collision of Heaven and Earth Leader's Guide
Steven L. Case
RETAIL $14.99
ISBN 978-0-310-28774-2

Visit www.planetwisdom.com or your local bookstore.

You are here for a reason. God is calling you to change the world. How will you do that? Inside the pages of this book, you'll discover that God has definitely created you for a purpose, and you'll learn what that purpose is. So, dive in, explore who you are and what you're made to do—so you can change the whole world.

Leave a Footprint—Change the Whole World
Tim Baker
RETAIL $9.99
ISBN 978-0-310-28325-6

Everyone has secrets, but you don't have to live with your pain all alone. *Secret Survivors* tells the compelling, true stories of people who've lived through painful secrets. As you read stories about rape, addiction, cutting, abuse, abortion, and more, you'll find the strength to share your own story and start healing, and you may even discover how to help a friend in pain.

Secret Survivors
Real-Life Stories to Give You Hope for Healing
Jen Howver & Megan Hutchinson
RETAIL $12.99
ISBN 978-0-310-28322-5